# The

# Owen Family

# Letters

## Keith Richards Thackrey
## and Maureen Thackrey Lischke

HERITAGE BOOKS
2012

# HERITAGE BOOKS

*AN IMPRINT OF HERITAGE BOOKS, INC.*

**Books, CDs, and more—Worldwide**

For our listing of thousands of titles see our website
at
www.HeritageBooks.com

Published 2012 by
HERITAGE BOOKS, INC.
Publishing Division
100 Railroad Ave. #104
Westminster, Maryland 21157

Title page photo: Bertha Owen Bice and her family

International Standard Book Numbers
Paperbound: 978-0-7884-5392-2
Clothbound: 978-0-7884-9485-7

To Clarence and Mary Owen, the chroniclers of our family history, and to Jessie Dean Thackrey, the bridge between Clarence and Mary's sister, Bertha, and those of us alive today.

# Table of Contents

# Table of Illustrations

# Acknowledgements

This book was created jointly by Maureen Thackrey Lischke and Keith Thackrey. The letters were transcribed by Maureen and she wrote most of the notes. Keith added the other text, added to the notes, and assembled the rest of the material.

We would first and foremost like to thank our families for their patience, their support and their contributions and ideas; Maureen's husband Erv, and Keith's wife Jeanie, as well as his two daughters, Kit and Rebecca. Rebecca played an extra role in helping Keith work through his anger issues with various software products.

We would like to thank our Mother, Jessie, and our sister Sue for their knowledge and support. In addition we relied on knowledge from others in the family, particularly our cousin Mike Dean for his help with the family history.

We also owe a large debt to our other sister Janet Daugherty, and close friend and former neighbor Fred Beck for their experienced eyes as proofreaders.

Of course, above all, we and our readers owe a tremendous debt to Owen, Bice, and Dean hoarders, who over a century and a half preserved these treasures.

# Preface

## *The Treasure*

This story has several beginnings as it spans several generations of a family. In the grand tradition of chronological consistency, I will, therefore, start at the end. That is the point where I entered the story.

In 1999, my aunt, Dorothy Dean Heiser, died at the age of 92. She and her husband, Harold, had lived in the town of Woodland Park, Colorado. Harold had died several years earlier, leaving Dorothy with their "things." Somewhat compulsive people by nature, they grew up during the Great Depression; their tendency to hoard was matched only by that of the Smithsonian Institution.

As Dorothy and Harold had no children of their own, it fell to one of Dorothy's surviving sisters, Mary Josephine Dean Thiessen (called Jane by her family), and a number of her nieces and nephews, to sift through the collections of more than 90 years. My sister, Maureen Thackrey Lischke, and I, were among those nieces and nephews.

Dorothy and Harold had lived in a relatively small, one-story rambler, with a garage, a crawl space under the house, and a storage shed in the back. It was, therefore, surprising to find that the house contained more than the largest government warehouses. We had all been there before, so we were not completely unprepared, but the scope of this massive undertaking could not be fully appreciated, except in retrospect.

The most obvious manifestations of this hoarding were the books. The house was full of books, stacked three feet high. There were narrow pathways between the books, and occasional chairs or tables were free, but most were buried. The books were highlighted and contained comments written in the margins. Articles and clippings on relevant topics were inserted in the books, often decades after the books were printed, indicating that these books were not just gathering dust, but had been read, remembered, and referenced. We donated most of the books to the local library, which would have tripled in size, had they not sold most to raise funds.

Less immediately visible was the garage. It was full of tools and spare parts for cars, motorcycles, and jeeps, which Harold had owned and repaired himself. It was also full of broken appliances and equipment. One other item found in the garage was Harold. There was an urn containing his ashes, which Dorothy kept in the garage since that was where he had spent so much of his time. The storage shed contained all the china, silver, furniture, and items they had saved from their home when they lived in Tulsa, Oklahoma, some forty years previously. Clearly, the books were of more value to Dorothy and Harold than the china and silver.

Least visible of all, but most alarming, was the crawl space under the house. It was full of old tires, gas cans (most, but not all, empty), and paint cans, among other types of junk. Dorothy and Harold had never used guns, but had been given a rifle and ammunition by a relative, in order to protect themselves. They kept the rifle and the ammunition separate, storing the ammunition under the house, with the gas cans, paint cans, and tires. A spark would have easily converted the Rocky Mountains to the Rocky Crater.

It has been said that one person's trash is another person's treasure. In this case, the reverse was true. Dorothy and Harold's treasures were our trash. We filled four or five dumpsters with the things we didn't keep or donate. Among this trash was a placard that stated "Use it up! Don't throw it out! Make it do, or do without!" There were, however, even by our standards, treasures within the trash. The local shipping office was buried for several days with our requests to ship furniture, china, pictures, and books to our homes around the country.

Among those treasures were several boxes of papers. These fell to my sister, Maureen, to take home; to review and assess at a more leisurely pace, when the pressures of imminent and catastrophic explosion were not present. Maureen has been reviewing these, a little at a time, ever since.

About ten years after taking possession of these boxes, she came across the greatest treasure of the lot. It was a box of letters, written to and about members of our family, during the 19th Century. At this point, the story jumps back in time more than 200 years.

## The Family

The oldest letter in the box was sent on the occasion of the death of Bethiah Hayward Leach. Bethiah was born in 1780 in Bridgewater, Massachusetts, and died in 1841 in Eaton, New York. In 1804 she married Backus Leach in Page Middleborough Town, Massachusetts. Backus was born in 1782, also in Bridgewater. He was the fifth of six children of Ichabod Leach and Penelope Standish Cobb. Ichabod was a soldier in the Continental Army during the American Revolutionary War.

Penelope, not to be outdone by her husband, was the great-great granddaughter of Miles Standish, the Captain of the Army contingent on board the Mayflower, as well as John Alden and Priscilla Mullins, also passengers on the Mayflower. In a flourish of originality, her grandfather and father were also named Miles Standish, and her only child from her first marriage was Miles Cobb.[1]

Bethiah and Backus had nine children. The second was Abigail Howard, born in 1812 in Massachusetts. In 1843, Abigail married Jason Owen in New York. Jason was born in 1805 in New York. The Owen family is less well documented than the Leach family, though from the letters, it is apparent that Jason had two brothers Stephen and Josiah, and possibly a sister. Abigail and Jason apparently had three children, all born in Lebanon, New York. Jason had a fourth child, Mortimer Warren who was the oldest, born in 1831 and was called Warren by his family. His mother, Phebe W. died in 1836, and is buried in Lebanon, New York. Henry Clarence was born in 1844, and at the age of 17 enlisted in Company A of the 38th Infantry Regiment, Illinois.[2] At various times he went by Henry, Clarence, Henry Clarence, and HC, but he most often used Clarence. Chloe Bethiah was born in 1846. She went by the name Bertha with her family and friends, and is apparently the only one of Abigail's three children to have children of her own. The last child of Jason and Abigail, Mary E. Owen was born in 1849. She was sometimes called Mate by her family and friends. The family moved to Elkhart, Illinois in 1856. Mary moved to Golconda, Illinois in the late 1860s to teach.

Bertha married Benjamin Franklin Bice in 1867. He went by BF or Frank, but is normally referred to as Frank in the letters. Frank enlisted in Company D of the Illinois 77th Infantry Regiment.[3] Bertha and Frank had nine children, the fourth of whom was Eva Logan (having been born in Logan County, Illinois). Eva was born in 1873 and married John Gillette Dean in 1897.

Eva and John raised their family in Homewood, Kansas. They had six children. In order, they are Bertha Elizabeth, Evelyn E., Dorothy T., Mary Josephine, Jessie Gertrude (my mother will kill me when she finds out I told you her middle name is Gertrude), and John Gillette Jr.

---

[1] From the "Descendants of John Alden and Priscilla Mullins",
http://www.alden.org/aldengen entry number 1605.
[2] Historical Data Systems, comp. *American Civil War Soldiers* [database on-line]. Provo:
The Generations Network, Inc., 1999. Copyright 1997-2000. Historical Data Systems, Inc.
[3] Historical Data Systems, comp.. *U.S. Civil War Soldier Records and Profiles* [database
on-line]. Provo: The Generations Network, Inc.. 2009.

Jessie married Franklin Thackrey in 1935, and also had six children, Janet, Karen, Kent Dean, Maureen, Sue, and Keith Richards. At last we get back to me. At the time of this writing, Jessie is the only surviving sibling. She remembers Bertha Owen Bice, who lived for several months with each of her children in rotation, until her death in 1927.

## *The Letters*

I have tried to give a short background to help put the letters in context, but the letters are the heart of this story; my writing just a poor diversion by comparison. There are a total of 88 letters. The first was written in 1841, the last in 1906. A little less than half of the letters, 34 total, were written by Clarence, from his campaigns in the Civil War. Another 16 were written by Mary, from Golconda. All of the letters were written, either to Jason and Abigail, or to Bertha. They all ended in the possession of Bertha, who passed them to her daughter Eva. Eva then passed them to her daughter Bertha Elizabeth. Elizabeth went by the name Bertha as a child, but started using Elizabeth during World War I, when the gun "Big Bertha" became famous. Elizabeth gave the letters to her sister Dorothy, where they stayed until found by Dorothy's niece, Maureen. In addition to the Owen family letters, there were several poems sent by Clarence to his family. Most were popular songs, but two poems seem to be original works, and are included.

The letters are grouped into five sections. The first section contains the letters sent before the Civil War. The second are the letters from and about Clarence during the War. The third group are those after the War, before the letters from Mary. The fourth are the letters from and about Mary, and the last group are those sent after the Golconda letters.

The letters were transcribed as faithfully as possible. The grammar and spelling are from the original letters. Many of the authors did not use punctuation, or used far less than we use today. There are places where the original letters have faded past the point that they are legible, but for the most part, the letters are in remarkably good condition.

There are notes after many of the letters explaining names and events when they are known. Much of the information came from the website www.ancestry.com though some came from other websites. Much of the family information either came from other families' trees, or from U.S. Census information, though some came from birth and marriage records, or from military service records.

The letters are written in Bookman Old Style font and use an 11 point font size. The rest of the book, including the notes, is written in Times New Roman font using a 10 point font size. All maps are taken from the Library of Congress web site http://memory.loc.gov on Military Battles and Campaigns. Individual citations are given with the maps.

*Keith R. Thackrey*

Map Legend (used for the maps throughout):

 Denotes a location from which a letter was sent

 Denotes the location where letters were received

# Introduction

Above the village of Elkhart, Illinois, hidden in the woods, lies the Elkhart Cemetery. Near the back of the cemetery, in the center, close to the small chapel, stands a gravestone of polished granite (second from the left of the four closest markers). The names on the gravestone are Jason Owen and Abigail H. "his wife." At the top of the stone it says "FATHER" and "MOTHER", and at the bottom it states "In life devoted In death united."

Farthest to the right of the four closest markers is a concrete obelisk which bears the following:

HENRY C.
son of
J. & A. H.
OWEN

On an adjacent face it states:

MARY E.
daut. of
J. & A. H.
OWEN

# Chapter 1 — Before the War

Warner, Higgins & Beers, et al. *Atlas of Kendall Co. and the state of Illinois: to which is added an atlas of the United States*, 1870. p. 23.

Highlighted City: Elkhart, Illinois

**Figure 1 — Illinois**

These letters introduce the Owen family. They were written to Jason and Abigail, from Abigail's cousin, Jason's niece, Jason's brother, and Abigail's father. The first letter predates Clarence, Bertha, and Mary. The rest were written when the three younger children were still small, Mary was eleven for the last letter.

\*\*\*\*\*\*\*\*\*\*\*\*\*\*\*\*\*\*\*\*\*\*\*\*\*\*\*\*\*\*\*\*

Easton May 29 1841

My dear afflicted friend & cousin.

The sad and unexpected intelligence of your mothers death awakened the tenderest sensibility of my heart – could sympathy alleviate your sorrow you have my deepest but alas! weak & inefficient is the deepest sympathy when our dearest friends are removed by death – nothing short of an Almighty arm can support and console in such an hour

When a mother is taken the affliction seems doubled – she who sustained us in infancy – guided us through childhood and youth up to riper years to when we always flew in difficulty or distress for advice & assistance – on whose opinion and judgment we relieded in the thousand little daily occurrences of life – with whom we have set around the domestic fireside -- walked to the house of God in company – mingled in the social circle – indeed almost every spot on which the eye can rest seems identified with her person – her name is wound up in the tenderest fibres of the heart the mention of which awakens every tender sensibility

The thought that such an one is gone never more to return to shine and animate a solitary hour or watch beside our sick bed is overpowering – Happy they who feel that they have an Almighty Friend to support & sustain through such an affliction – this – I

2

doubt not is your high privilege & may the removal of
your beloved mother be made up by the nearer &
dearer manifestations of your God & savior – May your
Fathers health be speedily restored & be precious in
his right who alone is able to continue it    I must ask
your pardon for my neglect in writing – I had been
laboring under the mistaken idea that you had not
answered my last – reading your former letter however
convinced me – I had been thinking of writing for some
time. Think not that you or your departed mother
have been forgotten – by no means – we have often
thought & spoken of you & heard she had regained
her usual health. To you we are permitted to make
this confession & assurance – but for her it seems too
late. Another addition to that page of events which so
loudly proclaims the danger of delay
        Her life was spared to accomplish an object she
ardently desired – vis – that of visiting the land of her
Fathers & the friends of her early years. I have often
thought of the gratification she appeared to feel on
being granted the privilege after which it seems her
health declined till she sunk in death      Mother has
often expressed fear that her journey was too much
for her slender health  But no doubt all things were
wisely ordered & so as to conduce most to her
happiness while here -- & the thought that she is
removed from all sin & sorrow to that land – where the
inhabitants shall no more say – I am sick is truly
comforting – and though you miss – and long will –
her endearing society let this consideration console &
comfort you in every sad & lonely hour. How transient
and fleeting our stay on Earth – a few short years and
we are gone – truly.

        "Lifes little stage is a small eminence
        Inch high the grave above, that home of man

Where dwells the multitude: we gaze around;
We read their monuments, we sigh; and while
We sigh we sink; and are what we deplored;
Lamenting, or lamented, all our lot"

Grant us an interest in your prayers that we
may be prepared – all of us – for the solemn event of
death – that so it may prove a welcome messenger
"Blessed indeed are those servants whom their Lord
when he cometh shall find watching"
We shall be gratified with a visit from your
Brother & wife – wish you and your Father would
come with them – Your friends in Easton I believe are
in comfortable health – Old Uncle & Aunt Hayward are
still living – she is able to attend meeting. Uncle
Edward's daughter – Rhoda who was married soon
after you were here died suddenly last November with
throat-ail  She was calm and resigned – ready and
willing to go – You inquired respecting Lydia Howard. I
have recently heard she had gone to her Fathers by
the way of Connecticut – where the Parents of Mr
Aekley (who is I am told her intended) – reside -- He
accompanied her He is a widower – she resided in his
family I think she was there when you were here. He
buried a child at that time – has four living – a great
undertaking – truly – she came to visit us last summer
– we were both absent – for which we were sorry –
have not seen her since. Should you see her tell her
we hope she will not be discouraged from coming
again. I have the privilege of informing you of the
comfortable health of our families who desire their
regards to you   Father & Mothers particular regards
to you. Father assuring him of their sympathy   Write
as soon as convenient.   Affectionately your friend

Susan H Copeland

PS you will see I have been waiting some time for a chance to mail this

Notes: The dashes in this letter do not reflect letters or words that I couldn't make out as is often the rule in other letters. Rather, it is the custom of this author to use dashes liberally – especially in place of a comma or a period. The letter was folded and on the outside of the back of one of the pages was written the address and postmarked, rather than being put in an envelope. It was addressed to Miss Abigail H Leach Eaton New York. The postmark is faded but it looks as though it says Boston and the date is some time in June.

Susan Copeland was the daughter of Susanna Hayward (1773–1859) and Josiah Copeland. Susanna'a brother was Edward Hayward (born around 1783) and his daughter was Rhoda Hayward Bartlett (1808–1840). Susanna's sister was Bethiah Hayward Leach (1780–1841). Susanna, Bethiah and Edward were the children of Edward and Susanna Hayward.

\*\*\*\*\*\*\*\*\*\*\*\*\*\*\*\*\*\*\*\*\*\*\*\*\*\*\*\*\*\*\*\*

Albany Apr 4th 1856

Dear Uncle and Aunt

I now take my pen to answer your welcomed and long looked for letter. but I can excuse you this time for when there is sickness in a family there is enough to think of without writing. I am glad that you have recovered your healths but I am afraid that the west will make you sick again it was very sickly there last Summer. but it may be more healthy this [time?]. I am sorry to here that you are going so far off I am afraid it will be a great while before we shall see each other again I have been in hope that we should meet before long if we all lived but now it looks rather dark unles you can come here before you go west. you could take the cars at Utica and run down here in a

little while then take the cars here and go clear
through to Buffalo, I wish you would but I suppose
you would think you could not. I cannot bare the
thoughts of your going off so far but perhaps it is all
for best we can write back and forth just as well and
perhaps see each other again my husband talks as if
he should go west if he should ever settle on a farm
but it is not likely to be very soon not as long as
business continues good here. we thank you both for
the kind inter you take in us and should we ever come
to Ill we should be glad of some friends. I hope you will
all find it what you anticipate and much more. we was
out to Uncle John Owens last January they wer all
well and mother also. Uncle Alouson Beach is a going
to start for Iowa the midle of this month his family will
not go untill fall he and his oldest son went out there
last fall and liked it here vary much. I donot know but
my friends will all get off to the west yet. You say that
Lebanon has changed vary much. I would rely like to
see the place once more but when you leave there,
there will be no object for me to go there it is a great
chance if I ever get there again. you did not say any
thing about Uncle Stevens folks. I would like to see
them vary much. and how I would like to see Clarence
and the girls but I should not know them it is no ways
likely. the rest of the friends has forgotten me there
has none of them ever written to me. and my old
mates there has none of them ever written to me but
Anvernette Sabin and Mary Norton. I answered their
letter and they never wrote again. I have tried to get
Cepas to write but he says he cannot think of any
thing to write that would be interesting he joins with
me in his respects to you. pleas excuse a poor letter
give my respects to all the friends and tell Warren I
think he mite write to us. and when you get to your
new home you must be shure and write for I shall be

anxious to here from you I have not wrote to each one
separately but ment it for both To my much respected
Aunt and Uncle A. H. and J. Owen
Pleas except this from your affectionate Niece

Mary L Hughson

Notes: This was in the same envelope that contained the letter
from Stephen Owen written from Lebanon Aug 20th 1856 and the
envelope is addressed to Jason Owen Williamsville Sangamon Co. Ill.
The postmark is Eaton NY dated Jun 23rd.
A. H. and J. Owen are Abigail and Jason Owen. "Clarence and
the girls" refers to Abigail and Jason's children. Uncle Steven is Stephen
Owen, brother of Jason. I haven't been able to find out more about
Jason's family so am not sure to whom Mary was related.
This was apparently written just prior to Jason and Abigail's
move from Lebanon, New York, to Williamsville, Illinois.

*******************************

Lebanon August 20 1856

Dear Brother
I have been verry negligent in answering your
letter but I hope that you will forgive and answer this
soon for we have not heard much from you since you
wrote our family are all well I am left alone to day they
have all gone to commencement to Hamilton it has
been verry Dry here this summer it rained yesterday a
little and today it is a raining finly corns is nothin
backward the Drouth having us later saved grain
haying and harvesting is pirty much through with but
the great topic here is about the outrages committee
in the halls of congress and in Cansas the peoples
seem to be Aversing in mass thanee one a few —
hunkins but a few in this town it will give a pirty clean
sweeps for Fremont in Hamilton usllay thosie same

7

fifty but thay are verry confident that Buchanan will be elected but it is my opinion according to present Affianance that the state of newyork will give fifty thousand majority for Fremont I feel that our liberties are pirty much taken from us but I hope that out of so much evil god will bring great  D—al of good Josiah and all came to our house one weeks last Saturday and my wife —ed him up to Ant shelia the old lady has been verry sick for a few days she looks verry poor now Horace Campbels folks are all well Dear Brother I feel verry lonely for I have no brother to visit now it come sometimes that if i should got to land hollow I should see you but Dear Brother and sister Da remember us an rite to us all about the plan and how you feel and the children and how you like and what you are a Doing but I must close and give my wife a chance this from your effetionat Brother

Stephen Owen

\*\*\*\*\*\*\*\*\*\*\*\*\*\*\*\*\*\*\*\*\*\*\*\*\*\*\*\*\*\*\*\*\*\*

August 24

I left a place for her to rite but she did not wan to and so i will give you a few lines more Trove Siles was a going to commencement on wednesday last  he turned over his Carriage near Andrew Beaches when taken up thought was dead but he so far recovered that he went home on friday the don't rain if this infleuat [influenza?] dos not set in that he will get along soon I saw Mister Casken yesterday he was well and sent his respects to you and wife I was over to ther hollow the fore part of the summer Horace has got the barn raised up and had got a picket fence the house west on the —d and he had began to paint the house I under stand the —in in the —all—s last night want a

going to get together and destroy the li-k— in the t— I
have not heard how thay — so I must bid you good
night

Stephen Owen


Notes: I apologize for this one – his spelling is terrible and so is
his handwriting, grammar and punctuation so I really had a difficult time.
This was in an envelope addressed to Jason Owen in
Williamsville Sangamon Co. Ill with a postmark of Eaton N.Y. However
the date is Jun 23. There is a second letter in the same envelope dated
Apr 4th 1856 from Albany to Dear Aunt and Uncle and signed Mary L
Hughson.
Stephen is Jason's brother. Stephen was born in 1795 and his
wife was Mary. They had a daughter, Helen C. Owen, born in 1830 and
they lived in Lebanon, New York for many years, but moved to
Hamilton, New York by 1860, where they lived with Helen and her
husband, Joseph Curtis. Helen and Joseph had a daughter, Louisa Smith
Owen, born in 1859, and sons Charles (born in 1856) and Edward (born
in 1850). Josiah Owen was born in 1790 in New Hampshire. His wife
was Sarah R. Owen, born in 1800. Their children were Sarah A. (born in
1828), Phebe E. (born in 1836) and Alvah H. (born in 1832). By 1830,
they also were living in Lebanon, New York.

*******************************

Eaton November 10th 1860

Distant and affectionate children I now sit down
to write to you to let you know that we have not
forgotton you we received your letter the next day after
I wrote to you it informed us that you got home well
and found the folks all well and that you was teaching
school in your district at 45 dollars per month. we are
all in tolerable good health and in pretty good spirits
our election went pretty strong for Lincoln and I
suppose if they elect a president in your state that you
will be so pleased without that you will not think of us

very soon. you wrote in your letter that you wanted me to send the date of that note the date of the note is June 18th 1859

the weather has been very wet we have had but a little fair weather they did not finish digging potatoes until yesterday. Our school commenced this week the little fox teaches. our folks are very busy affixing Terressas things to go to school at Utica the Term begins the 20 of this month so that they are pretty full of businiss at present we want you to write what Mr. Hamilton is doing and how he gets along and how he likes and how the people like him and what ways he gets and where he is teaching I must draw to a close by styling myself your father A J Leach

Backus Leach

\*\*\*\*\*\*\*\*\*\*\*\*\*\*\*\*\*\*\*\*\*\*\*\*\*\*\*\*\*\*\*

Mr Owen and family

Distant and affectionate children I sit down to write to you to let you know that we have not forgotten you though we have not heard from you in particular for some time when A J wrote he wrote that he got home well and found the people all well. we are usually well. yesterday was stormy and to day it is stormy so that we did not go to meeting it snows some and is wet and muddy. we should be glad to have you write and let un know how you are at this time for I expect you are all in good spirits at this time but I must stop. your father Esq Hoppin continues to be deranged and does not get any better

Backus Leach

\*\*\*\*\*\*\*\*\*\*\*\*\*\*\*\*\*\*\*\*\*\*\*\*\*\*\*\*\*\*\*

Daniel S Leach and family
Distant and affectionate children I take my pen to write to you I hardly know how to addressy you for we donot hear from you only by other folks whether you have forgotton us or whether you are so drove in business we cannot tell but we want you to show us with a letter that it is neither we are in comfortable health and I suppose you are in great glee thinking that you have a president in your own state and can split your own rails whether you have any timber or not Mother and Terressa send their love to all enquiring friends this from your affectionate father Backus Leach

Notes: These 3 letters were all on the same piece of paper. A J is Adoniram Judsow Leach. Backus Leach is the father of Adoniram Judsow, Daniel Standish, Henry Howard, Terressa Chloe, Augustin, Horatio, Chloe H., Mirretta (Mary), and Abigail H. Leach (who married Jason Owen). Daniel Standish is the Daniel S. addressed in the third letter.

The Owen Family lived in Williamsville, Illinois, at this time. Williamsville is about 15 miles from Springfield. There has been no indication that the Owen Family ever met Mr. Lincoln, but to Backus, who lived in New York, it must have seemed as if his daughter Abigail and Mr. Lincoln were next door neighbors, and to the Owen Family, it was a case of "local boy makes good."

# Chapter 2 — The Civil War Letters of Henry Clarence Owen

## Missouri and Arkansas

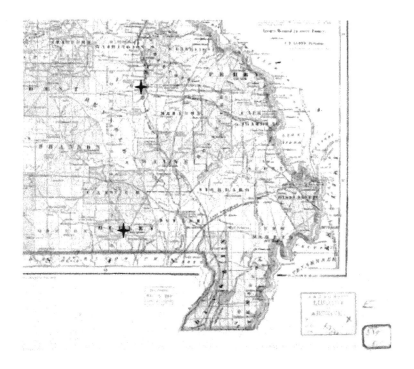

James T. Lloyd, *Lloyd's official map of Missouri Drawn and engraved from actual surveys for the Land Office Department*, New York: J. T. Lloyd, 1861. Number 296.2.

Highlighted Cities (north to south): Pilot Knob, Doniphan

**Figure 2 — Missouri**

Henry Clarence Owen, who went by Henry, Henry Clarence, HC, or most often Clarence, enlisted as a private on July 15, 1861, at the age of 17. On August 19, 1861 he enlisted in Company A of the newly formed 38th Infantry Regiment Illinois.[4] His handwriting was very good. His punctuation, spelling, and grammar, not so much.

The Regimental Commander of the 38th was Col. William Passmore Carlin. Carlin wrote memoirs of his military service, which were published.[5] These memoirs, along with a National Park Service website[6] on the U. S. Civil War filled in gaps in the letters regarding the movements of the 38th Regiment, provided background, and helped with names, places, and battles that were difficult to figure out due to spelling, faded writing, or errors.

Clearly, from the letters, getting stamps was an issue for the soldiers.

*********************************

Oct 6th 1861

Dear Father

I now take my pen to let you know that I am well at present there has nothing of importance happened here yet we are expecting an attack from hardee and we are very well prepared to meet him we have one regiment of infantry and four hundred of cavalry here at pilot knob and at Ironton there is two regiments of infantry and they are building a fort there I went up to Ironton last sunday and I saw John Jones a lawyer [inkblot wiped out one word] and several more boys from our neighborhood they were all well and in good spirits they told me that they had been all over missouri but could not get the rebbels to fight them we have had a few prisoners here

---

[4] Historical Data Systems, comp., *U.S. Civil War Soldier Records and Profiles*
[5] Robert I. Girardi and Nathaniel Cheairs Hughes, Jr., editors, *The Memoirs of Brigadier General William Passmore Carlin, USA*, Lincoln: University of Nebraska Press, 1999.
[6] National Park Service. *Civil War Soldiers and Sailor System*, http://www.itd.nps.gov/cwss/regiments.cfm.

but have let the most of them go again we have one reg at Ironton working on the fort I helped take one man here in town yesterday after we had taken him he first said he belonged to the south then he said afterwards said that he belonged to the home guards and was in the three months service we had a very hard rain here yesterday and last night the rain blew in to the tents and the boys got as wet as they could be I happened to be on guard before the majors tent and he let me stand in his tent so that i did not get wet till I was going from where we staid to my post i got my feet wet Reuben received a letter from home the other day and they wrote that John Lindsay had come home but was going to enlist again the times are very hard here we have not received any pay yet and we are out of money so that I cannot get any postage stamps that is one reason why I have not written before the report was last night that there was fifteen hundred rebbels with in three miles of here the boys laid on their guns all night ready to receive them but they have not come yet our company is going up to Ironton tomorrow to raise the cannon in the fort I received a letter from warren a few days before we left camp butler he wrote that they were all well there is preaching over in the cavalry tonight I don't think of any thing more at present direct your letters to company A 38th reg Ill vol

H C Owen

Miss Ida M Leach
PS direct pilot knob Iron co mo
Monday morning we had to lay on our arms last night yesterday we received news that there was a company of rebbels within eight miles of here they sent four hundred cavalry out and the last we heard from them they had taken Talbot and sixty men and there was

seven hundred secesh was cavalry after them I have to artillery drill now

Notes: This is on stationery with a picture of a woman holding the US flag in her right hand and a sword in her left.

Ironton, Missouri is south of St. Louis, between St. Louis and Cairo. Pilot Knob, Missouri is near Ironton.

The 38th Regiment Illinois Volunteers (Infantry) were organized at Camp Butler, Illinois and mustered in Aug. 15, 1861. It was to have been for 3 years. However, they were not mustered out until Dec. 31, 1865. They were ordered to Pilot Knob, Missouri on Sept. 20, 1861 and were on duty there until March 1862. They were attached to the Department of Missouri until March 1862.

Reuben (Rube) is Reuben Lightfoot, also from Sangamon County, Illinois. Clarence refers to him in several letters.

Ida Leach was the daughter of Abigail Leach's brother, referred to as Uncle Howard. So Ida was a cousin of Clarence's.

*******************************

McLean Ills Oct 29 1861

Dear Parents

Having waited a long time for an answer to my letter I thought I had better answer it myself or it would not perhaps be answered at all, when I wrote you last I told you that I wanted to build me a house (or shanty rather) have done so and been living in it something over two months. I built on the corner opposite where James lived I bought me two lots on the corner for Eighty Dollars the same two that James bought and had broke the first summer he lived there and was to give Two Hundred & Twenty Dollars for them so you will see that town lots are a little lower my House is 16 x 24  9 ft Posts boarded up and down and battened cottage style have a kitchen two bed rooms a clothes press and Pantry closet so that we can get along very comfortable and in the Spring I want to build me a rough kitchen on back one that

will answer for a summer kitchen and for a wood &
Store room in the winter and now would be very glad
to have you come up and see us in our new home, We
did intend to have come down and made you a visit
this fall but have had to give it up as I can not raise
enough of the needful to so with building and a
kindness of James it has left me rather short, and
now Father I must tell you how James served me. Last
May he was here to see me and I went up to
Bloomington with him on some business, while there
Mr Funk took him with a Capais [caprice?] on some old
wheat matters of Owen & Laderus and was bound
either to have some money or put him to Jail, after
talking with him a long Funk told James if I would
give him my Notes one for Twenty five dollars payable
within one year the other for the same amount
payable within two years to be taken out of the Store
at such times as he should see fit he would release
him, after talking with James he said if I would do so
he would send me five dollars every two months till
the notes were paid and so I gave the notes at the
same time James told me that he came from Chicago
and forgot his money and had not enough to get him
back to Chicago and said if I would let him have some
money he would sent it down to me the next day so I
let him have Eight dollars, but as yet have not
received one cent of it yet or on the notes either. I
received one letter from him about two weeks after he
left here, and after I have written to him about the
borrowed money and he said he had sent the money
and said he had rented the Fulton House in Fulton
City I answered his letter immediately telling him the
money had not come and have since wrote two more
but get no answers and the last one has come back to
me. so it will seem he is not at Fulton and where he is
I do not know but enough of this.

I received a letter from Camp Butler about a month ago I suppose from Clarence, as whoever wrote it forgot to sign their name I answered the letter the next day but have not heard anything more from him when you write me I wish you would give me the number of his Regiment also his Company the name of his Captain and where they are so I can write him again. Abby and the children are usually well. Willis goes to school every day and likes it very much Abby joins with me in sending love to all and says be sure to write them to come up and see us, as my paper is full I shall have to close.

Affectionately your son Warren

Notes: This was in an envelope addressed to Jason Owen Esq Williamsville Sangamon County Illinois with a postmark that was cut out but the remaining part says Ill.

There is a US flag on the envelope and it says "Then conquer we must, for our cause it is just, And this be our motto 'In God is our trust,' And the Star-spangled banner in triumph shall wave O'er the land of the free and the home of the brave."

Warren Owen is the brother of Clarence. James' identity is not clear. It is possible he was married to a close family friend, Sarah Camel, who lived with the Owen family during the 1850 Census .

\*\*\*\*\*\*\*\*\*\*\*\*\*\*\*\*\*\*\*\*\*\*\*\*\*\*\*\*\*\*\*\*

Pilot Knob Dec 22nd 1861

Dear Sisters
I take my pen to let you know that I am well at present We have had very warm pleasant weather the most of the time this fall while Rube was at home we had two or three inches of snow but it did not last but three days it has been dry  ever since untill yesterday it commenced snowing and it snowed all day and it turned to sleet in the night and this morning our tent was covered with ice to day it is snowing again we

drawed a new uniform a week ago yesterday and we got brass should [I think he meant shoulder] scales and the letter of our company Company A and Company H have got end field rifles there is nothing new to write I do not know when I shall come home the colonel will not give any furloughs at present Rube sends his best respects I do not think of any thing more to write at present from your Brother H C O

Notes: This was written on stationery that has a picture of a woman with a laurel wreath on her head holding a sword in one hand and a US flag in the other and it says Death to Traitors under her feet.

The 38th had operations around Fredericktown, Missouri, Oct. 12–15, 1861 and then an expedition against Thompson's forces Nov. 2–12.

The "end field rifles" are actually the British manufactured Enfield rifled muskets. These were the second most numerous small arms in the Union army during the Civil War.

********************************

Pilot Knob Feb 2 1862
Dear Father I take my pen to let you know that I am well at present we have every thing ready to leave here tomorrow our destination I do not know we will go to greenville first and probably from there to Pocahontas and then to New Madrid we got orders to leave every thing but one suit so I thought I would box up what I could not carry and send them home I got a letter from warren the other day the folks are all well he has bought Ladew out and is carrying the store on by himself and I got one from Horatio he said that uncle howard was drawing ice to the city for 75 cts a load I was in hopes that I would get a chance to come home in a few days but there is no chance now there is nothing more to write at present tell the girls I will write to them when we come to a stopping place

mother wanted to know what those green spots on that sketch were. they are intended to represent the rocks and the building on the knob is where they got the ore tell mary that those things twisted together with wire are the kind of caps that we used with the guns that we got when we first come here but we have got better guns now nothing more at present
from your son    H. C. Owen

Notes:  Pilot Knob is in Missouri, as is Greenville. Pocahontas is in Arkansas, in the Northeast corner, on the Black River, just south of Doniphan, Missouri, and between Doniphan and Jacksonport, Arkansas. In his memoirs, then Col. Carlin reported that the mission to Pocahontas was a secret mission, about which only he and Lt. Hoekl in the 38th had any knowledge. Col. Carlin was rebuked by his commander, Maj. Gen. H. W. Halleck, for leaking information about this mission.[7] He claimed it was an unjust rebuke, driven by politics. Whether the information got to Clarence through a leak from Carlin or Hoekl, through guess work, or through a leak from Halleck's Headquarters is speculation, but clearly others in the 38th had knowledge of the mission, which never took place.

Warren is Mortimer Warren Owen, Clarence's older half-brother, who was born in 1831. Uncle Howard probably is Henry H. (also known as Howard) Leach, 1814–1892, and the brother of Clarence's mother. Horatio was the son of Uncle Howard and the brother of Ida (mentioned in the Oct 6, 1861 letter) and thus a cousin of Clarence's. Ida and Horatio were about the same age as Clarence and Bertha.

*******************************

Feb 3rd 1862
Dear Father  I take my pen to let you know that I am well at present there is nothing new going on here now the 21st reg has gone to pocahontas there was about six inches of snow the morning that they left they had

---

[7] Girardi and Hughes, *The Memoirs of Brigadier General William Passmore Carlin USA*, pp. 38–40.

not got out of sight of their camp before they had to
wade in the water up to their arms I am going to send
a box by express to day with a picture of our company
for the girls and some specimens of ore and sinder
from the furnace I have no more to write at present so
good bye   from your son

H C Owen

Notes:   This stationery has a picture of a Union soldier at
attention holding a rifle with bayonet in front of a tent with a US flag and
a cannon and three rifles standing up on the ground making a pyramid
and it says "Our Union Defenders."

\*\*\*\*\*\*\*\*\*\*\*\*\*\*\*\*\*\*\*\*\*\*\*\*\*\*\*\*\*\*\*\*

Feb 4th 1862
Dear Sisters  I am well at present I received a letter
from mother today and was glad to hear that you were
all well. there is some talk of our leaving here before
long and going to pocahontas that is over one hundred
miles from here it is in arkansas they are talking of
opening a line from there to Pocahontas the 21st is in
greenville now and the 33rd is going to Pitmans Ferry
well no more about what we are going to do now the
cap bought a can of oysters and we have just had
supper I live fine here we have beef steak mutton ham
prairie chickens rabbits and everything that is game I
am excused from all duty while I am cooking I have to
make Biscuit twice a day there is talk in camp of our
declaring war against great Britton and if they do you
need not look for me home for a good while tell mother
that she need not be scared if I do not come home
next spring nothing more at present write as soon as
you get this letter and let me know if you have got that
box and if every thing is safe
        from your Brother H C O

21

Notes: This letter was written in red ink and the stationery has a picture of a Union soldier holding a US flag and it says "One Flag, One Country"

Pitmans Ferry is actually Putman's Ferry, Missouri.

\*\*\*\*\*\*\*\*\*\*\*\*\*\*\*\*\*\*\*\*\*\*\*\*\*\*\*\*\*\*\*\*\*\*

Doniphan Apr 6th 1862

Dear Sister it is with pleasure that I take my pencil to let you know that I am well at present and I hope these few lines will find you well we are now at Donsiphan Riply Co about 100 miles south of the knob we will probably stay here 10 days then go to Pocahontous it has been most two months since I have had a letter from you I wrote a letter to you first before we left the knob but have received no answer yet I want you should write as soon as you get this letter and let me know how you all are there was about 80 rebels here when the cavalry came up they exchanged a few shots with our boys and then ran our cavalry killed one lieut there was none of our men hit they lie around in the woods and fire on our pickets once in a while but they have not hit yet. the other night just before roll call they fired on the pickets and raised the alarm in camp we was all out in line in a very few minutes the rebels still fired again once in a while out side of the Pickets our Battery went down to the edge of the river and throwed one shell over about where they thought the rebels were and we heard no more from them that night the cavalry are bringing in Prisoners all the time Two companies went to Pitmans Ferry yesterday that is about 10 miles down the river and they carry hot old Pitman I have nothing more to write at present from your Brother

H. C. Owen

# The Owen Family Letters

Notes: This was in the same envelope as the Jul. 11, 1864 letter. In Mar., 1862, the 38th was attached to the 1st Brigade, Steele's Army of S.E. Missouri until June, 1862. They moved to Reeve's Station on the Black River Mar. 3–10, 1862. Doniphan is in Ripley County, Missouri, near the Arkansas border. The knob he is referring to is Pilot Knob. Both towns are in the eastern part of Missouri. The 38th moved to Doniphan and Pocahontas Mar. 31–Apr. 21. They had action at Putman's Ferry, Missouri, on Apr. 1.

*********************************

May 17th 1862

Dear Father

It is with pleasure that I take my pen to let you know that I am well at present we are in greenville now on the road to Cape Girardeau we left Jackson port the 10th and if we have good luck three days more will take us to the cape a distance of 200 miles I received your last letter at Pittmans ferry and you may be assured that I was glad to hear from you the reason why I have not wrote to you before is because we have been marching for the last two months and have had no opportunity to send a letter our 1st Lieut is going by the knob and I thought I would write a few lines to let you know where I was I hope I shall be at home before long so goodbye

from your son

Henry C. Owen

(PS) I will write to you again when we get to the cape

Notes: This is on stationery with the US flag in the left top corner in blue.

Greenville is in Missouri. Clarence calls it Pittmans ferry, but actually it is Putman's Ferry, Missouri.

The 38th moved to Jacksonport, Arkansas, Apr. 30–May 4 and then to Cape Girardeau, Missouri, May 10–21.

# Mississippi, Alabama, and Tennessee

Capt. N. Michler and Maj. J.E. Weyss, *Topographical sketch of Corinth, Mississippi and its environs: showing the enemy's entrenchments, and the approach of the U.S. forces,* 1862.

**Figure 3 — Corinth, Mississippi**

Sunday June 8th 1862

Dear Sister

It is with pleasure that I take this opportunity to let
you know that I am well at present we are about 15
miles from corinth now but there is no telling where
we will be by this time tomorrow night we got orders
this afternoon to cook three days rations and put
them in our haversacks I passed over a portion of the
battle ground at pittsburgh landing it was an awful
place the trees were riddled all to pieces with cannon
balls and musket balls I passed General Johnson's
grave there was stakes stuck around it we are under
Gen'l Popes command we are held in reserve and we
have to spend the rest of our time working on the
roads I never saw any body so disappointed in my life
as the boys were when the rebels left early for they
had made up their minds for a fight there and it
discouraged them so that several of them all most had
a mind to desert they all blame Hallock for letting the
rebels get out of there without a fight the rebels
managed it so nicely we never thought of their leaving
untill the morning that they left they kept a strong
front out all of the time the morning before they left
there was very hard fighting two hours once regiment
of the pea—tge boys come on to a lot of them about
three quarters of a mile in front of us and the muskets
rattled heavyer for a while than they did any of the
time fredricktown it is roll call now and I will have to
bring my letter to a close so no more at present from
your brother

Henry C Owen

(PS) Direct your letters to co a 38th reg Ill Vol in care of
Col Carlin Gen'l
Popes Army via corinth

Notes: Corinth is in northern Mississippi. Pittsburg Landing is in Tennessee, northeast of Corinth.

From Cape Girardeau, they took a hospital steamer down the Mississippi River to Cairo, up the Ohio River to Paducah, up the Tennessee River to Pittsburg Landing. From there, the 38th moved to Hamburg Landing, Tennessee, May 21–24 and then fought in the siege of Corinth, Mississippi, May 26–30, 1862. Then they engaged in a pursuit to Booneville May 31–June 12. In June, the 38th was attached to the 2nd Brigade, 4th Division, Army of Mississippi, until Sept.1862.

**********************************

General Davise's Division
2nd Brigade
Col Carlins comd
June 20th 1862

Dear Sister it was with with pleasure that I received your letter day before yesterday and I intended to answer it as soon as I came off of guard but I felt so unwell that I did not do any thing yesterday but lay in the shade and sleep we have Battallion drill two hours before breakfast and two hours in the afternoon and we have to clean our quarters up every morning and sweep all of the dirt away and it has to be done before breakfast there is a great many of the men sick almost half of our company is unfit for duty the water is very bad here and the days are warm and the nights very cold the lieut col has command of our regiment now he don't know any thing about drilling and he made a bad mistake yesterday morning and the boys commenced laughing at him and he says boys don't laugh at me for I don't know much about it any how
we are camped on clear creek now about four miles from corinth several of the boys have been there but I have not had any chance to go there yet but I mean to go in two or three days when you write again I want

27

you should when you commenced your school and
how many schollars you have and how far your school
is from mr Hopppins iff we stay here three or four
weeks I shall try to come home but there is no telling
where we will be in that time I saw Beck the other day
he has been promoted to corporal I don't know as
there is any thing more to write at present so good bye
from your brother

H C Owen
(PS) Direct your letters to Co "A" 38th reg General
Davise's Division in care of col Carlin

Note: Written upside down on the last page and over some of
the above letter is the following letter.

*******************************

Dear Pa and Ma June 6
I have just received a letter from Clarence. I thought
as there was a little space, I would write a few lines to
you and send it on. I have not heard a word from
home since Uncle was here I have wrote one letter
home but no answer. Libbie wrote that old Mr Taylor
was dead and Mr Sheldon Hitches wife is dead. Uncle
Howard; Aunt, and Chere [?] had gone to Onida. I am
getting along quite well with my school. Will you come
after me? I will send this letter home; thot I wrote to
Clarence as I do not know where to direct it
[one word I can't read] still at present write very soon good
bye
From your daughter. Love to all.
Bertha

Notes: The dates are confusing because Clarence's is clearly Jun. 20 and Bertha's is clearly Jun. 6 — one of them may have made a mistake as to what month it was. The end of Bertha's is also a little confusing since Clarence told her where to write.

Corinth is in Mississippi. The Beck Clarence refers to is George Beck and he was killed later in the war. General Davise is actually Gen. Jefferson C. Davis. The Lt. Col. he refers to is Mortimer O'Kean. Col. Carlin referred to him as being older, not good at tactics, and "made confusion at battalion drill."[8] O'Kean resigned before the year was out.

---

[8] Girardi and Hughes, *The Memoirs of Brigadier General William Passmore Carlin, USA.* p. 46.

# Kentucky and the Battle of Perryville

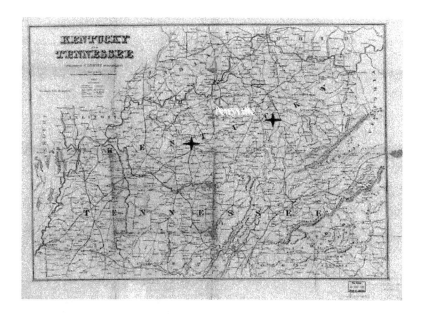

O. Lederle, *Kentucky and Tennessee*, Memphis: 1862.

Highlighted Cities (east to west): Crab Orchard, Bowling Green

**Figure 4 — Kentucky and Tennessee**

31st Brig
9th Division
Army of the Ohio

Camp near Crab Orchard

Sept 16th 1862

Dear Sisters I received your welcome letter at
Louisville but have had no time to answer it untill now
we have been marching ever since we were in the
battle of Perryville and have been in one or two
skirmishes since and there one of our men wounded
yet we were on a forced march all the way from
Jacinto to Louisville and when we got there we had to
put out after Bragg so you see we have had but very
little rest since the 14th of last Aug and there is no
telling when we will get any rest we have stopped here
for one day only I saw John Lanterman and Bill Bagus
the other day their reg is along with us. our reg
captured 16 wagons and 86 prisoners at Peryville
without firing a gun I receive a letter from Ida and one
from Horatio while we were at Louisville I believe that I
had better come home and go to teaching school for I
can make more at it than I can a soldiering and I am
sure that it is easier than marching all the time and
carry a knapsack besides. tell hulda that I have no
way of sending her a marble but when I come home I
will bring her one we were in Kentucky when they had
that fight at Iuka we have had no tents since the first
of July so we have to lay out and take the weather just
as it comes you would have to laugh if you were to see
me now sitting on the ground with my knapsack on
my knee for a writing desk
I don't think of anything more to write at present give
my love to all from your Brother

Henry C. Owen

Notes: This is on stationery with a Zouave soldier holding a US flag in his left hand and a sword in his right with a broken drum, broken sword and broken cannon at his feet and he is standing on a Confederate flag.

Crab Orchard is in Kentucky, as is Perryville. Iuka is in Mississippi, southeast of Corinth, Mississippi. The Siege of Corinth was Apr. 29–Jun. 10, 1862 and the Battle at Iuka was Sept. 20, 1862. Note he has addressed this as Sept. 16, 1862. I believe he had the month wrong and it should have been Oct. 16, 1862. Not sure who Hulda is. She was at school with Bertha at Normal, Illinois, but don't know if she was a friend or a relative.

From Jun. 29 to Jul. 4, the 38th marched to Jacinto and Ripley. They were in Corinth, Mississippi, until Aug. 14th. They then marched from Aug. 14–Sept. 26 through Alabama to Nashville, Tennessee, and then to Louisville, Kentucky, in pursuit of Bragg. They pursued Bragg into Kentucky, Oct. 1–16 and fought in the Battle of Perryville Oct. 8. They also were in Manchester and Stanford, Kentucky on Oct. 14th. They began their march to Nashville, Tennessee, on Oct. 16, arriving in Nashville on Nov. 9. During the month of Sept. the 38th was attached to the 31st Brigade, 9th Division, Army of the Ohio. Then during the month of Oct. they were with the 31st Brigade, 9th Division, 3rd Corps, Army of the Ohio.

**********************************

My home from b—nd
Bowling green
Nov 4th 1862

Dear Father I received your letter yesterday and was glad to hear that you were all well I received a letter from you while we were at Louisville but had no opportunity to answer it untill we got to crab orchard I have seen John Lanterman and Bill Bagus several times their Division is with us so that we can see each other when ever we want to we are now on our way to Nashville now we left John Lanterman in the hospital at Bowling green yesterday he was very sick but I think he will get better soon I received a letter from

33

Horatio at Louisville and was some what surprised to hear that he had enlisted but enough of this I will tell you a little about our travels through St. L. we fared very well untill after we got to Bowling green although we had to march hazed all the time our knapsacks were hauled for us and we had plenty to eat but after we got to Bowling green we had to live on half rations carry our knapsacks and march day and night to Louisville our crackers gave out and we had to use flour you would laughed if you could have seen us cooking it we took a Barrel and knocked the head in and then took a bucket of water and some salt put it in the barrel and mixed it up then put it in the ashes and cooked it that is the kind of bread we lived on for a week and very often they wouldn't gave us time to cook even enough of that so you can guess what soldiering is but I have stood it well I am hearty as I ever was in my life no more at present from your son
Henry C Owen

Notes: There is a note written at the bottom of the letter upside down that says "My friend by this no never come home."

Louisville, Crab Orchard, and Bowling Green are all in Kentucky. Buell gave up command at Bowling Green and Rosecrans assumed it.

The 38th arrived in Nashville Nov 9 and had duty there until Dec. 26. During Nov. and Dec. they were attached to the 2nd Brigade, 1st Division, Right Wing 14th Army Corps, Army of the Cumberland. The Army of the Ohio had its name changed to the Army of the Cumberland when Rosecrans assumed command in Oct. 1862.

## Tennessee and the Battle of Stones River (Murfreesboro)

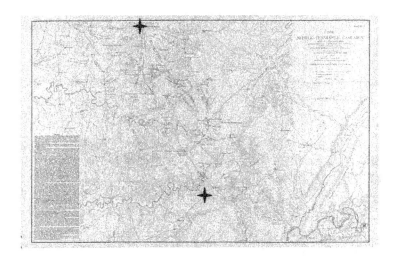

U.S. Army Corps of Engineers, *The Middle Tennessee and Chattanooga campaigns of June, July, August, and September 1863*, Map 1, by J. von Glümer, New York: Julius Bien & Co., 1891.

Highlighted Cities (north to south): Nashville, Winchester

**Figure 5 — Tennessee**

Nov 26th 1862

Dear Sister

I received your letter of the twelfth
day before yesterday and was glad to hear that you
were all well I am well at present we are camped three
miles from Nashville we have very pleasant weather at
present have had but very little rain this fall every
thing is very scarce here and brings a very high price
butter is worth from fifty cents to one dollar and beef
from 12 to 15 cents chickens from fifty to seventy five
cents eggs sixty cents so you can guess what it costs
to live here they have just got the railroad in operation
through to Louisville the train ran off the track the
other morning and smashed six passenger cars all to
pieces one man got his arm broke and another got his
leg broke there is considerable excitement here about
enlisting in the regular service three of our company
enlisted to day and there is several more talking of
enlisting but I think that this service is regular
enough for me without enlisting again Captain Alden
came to us about a week after we left crab orchard he
is well now you spoke about John Henry writing every
week if he was marching all of the time as we have
been I don't think he would write quite so often it is
most half of the time that we can postage stamps nor
paper and we cannot get them now when we get where
they are for we are out of money we have not been
paid for six months and there is very poor prospects of
our being paid very soon I got three letters at
Louisville that I have not answered yet I got one from
Ida that I have not answered yet I don't think of any
thing more at present from your brother

Henry C. Owen

(PS) Please send me some stamps when you write again

******************************

Nov 29th 1862

Dear sister I received your welcome letter the day before yesterday, and was very sorry to hear that Mary was sick I have not been well for two days but am feeling some better now Rube is well Mr Lanterman has not been able for duty for more than two weeks we are at Nashville but know not what time we may be ordered to leave here we have been marching ever since the 14th of Aug there is some talk of our staying here this winter. our reg't was out on a five days scout when we came back we brought fifty Prisoners about the same number of horses and several teems we caught one capt of a guerrilla company, his sentence is to work on fortifications during the war and twenty days close confinement every six months I don't think of any thing more at present I have answered every letter that I have received from home I wrote while we were at Crab orchard   from your Brother
H C Owen

******************************

Near Murfreesboro
Tennisee
Jan 6th 1863

Dear Sister

It is with pleasure that I take this opportunity of letting you know that I am well at present I received your letter before we left our old camp and the paper came after I wrote Dear Sister we have had one of the hardest fought battles here that has been fought since this war commenced we commenced fighting the twenty sixth and fought some every day untill the third of this month On the twenty sixth our regiment charged a battery and took one piece and the rest run be fore we got close enough to keep them from taking their guns with them. our company was deployed out in front of the regiment as skirmishers and we marched nearly a mile under the fire of that battery the shells bursting over our heads and all around us but there was not a man hurt in our company that day after that was over we all thought that we had seen a hard fight in fact it was the hardest fighting we had ever done but when we come to face the enemy here we found it a different thing alltogether the night of the thirtieth we lay within one hundred and fifty yards of the enemies lines had not a sign of a fire had to lay on the ground with no blankets and you may know that we got but very little sleep for it was so cold that we couldn't sleep but the next morning was when we had the severeist fighting to do that morning we had and we lost twenty six killed and wounded there was three regiments of rebels marching up right in front of us and they had already drove our men back on the right and were raking us from two ways I had heard men tell about being where it rained bullets but it come the mightest to it there of any place I have seen yet. Rube was wounded there in the arm and hand and has died since for the want of care I got out without a scratch the men fell in front and on both sides of me the enemy had the whole right wing of our army badly whiped that day they were scattered every where lots of our men run to Nashville before they stoped but we have finally whipped them at last our captain was wounded in both legs but nothing very serious and our orderly sergeant was hit in the right hand took the

end of his thumb three first fingers off I tell you they
are very careless how they shoot they had just as kill a
man as not and I mistrust that they think the same of
us we left our knapsacks and every thing we had in
the wagon and they were sent to Nashville and while
there they were unloaded and several of them robbed
they took a new dress coat that I had never wore any
and apair of pants and port folio I had nearly a dollars
worth of paper and envelopes and over a dollars worth
of stamps they didn't leave scarcely any thing I believe
there is nothing of importance now I would like to
have you send me some more stamps when you
answer this from your brother

Henry Owen

Notes: Their regiment was involved in the Battle of Stones
River (aka Murfreesboro) Dec. 30–31, 1862 and Jan. 1–3, 1863. That
was when the heaviest fighting occurred but from his letter, it appears
they were skirmishing before and after those dates.

The 38th stayed at Murfreesboro until Jun. 1863. In Jan. 1863,
they were attached to the 2nd Brigade, 1st Division, 20th Army Corps,
Army of the Cumberland until Oct. 1863. The 38th performed
reconnaissance from Murfreesboro Mar. 6–7 and went to Versailles Mar.
9–14. They had operations on the Edgeville Pike on Jun. 4.

Rube was Clarence's friend, Rueben Lightfoot, from Sangamon
County, Illinois. He died Jan. 5, 1863, from wounds received during the
Battle of Stones River.

*******************************

Jan 20th 1863
2nd Brigade 1st Division
Right Wing 14th Army
Corps

Dear Father

Not hearing from you for
some time I could not imagine what was the matter I
have not heard from you since before we left our camp

near Nashville although I have written three or four letters I did not know whether you had got them so I take this opportunity of writing again and to let you know that I am among the living Father our Brigade has been through one of the hardest battles that has ever been fought in the west on the morning of the 26th we received orders to strike tents and be ready to march at a moments warning with three days rations in our haver sacks at last the order came to march we started at 7 "o"clock a.m. about half past 8 it commenced raining and it rained two or three hours steady we had not gone more than three or four miles when the first Brigade commenced skirmishing, with the advance of Braggs army they skirmished for two or three miles when the rebels made a stand and we were drawn up in line and Co "H" were thrown in advance as skirmishers and they showed their bravery we went through a ceder grove and the skirmishers were shooting all the time and they couldn't see anything to shoot at they were so fraid that they did not keep out of the way of the reg't finally when we got nearly through this grove we saw some cavalry weave advanced in to an open field and we could see them riding around but out of reach of our guns they had two pieces of artillery about a quarter of a mile off they fired three or four rounds at us one shell bursting directly over the regiment and a solid shot struck just in front of us and rolled in to the ranks but no one was hurt there then Col Carlin came along gave the order to fix Bayonets then come to our company and told the captain that he wanted him to though [think he meant tough] his company out as skirmishers and charge that Battery and we started but the rebels started also we followed them nearly a mile they made a stand at what is called knob gap and we skirmished half a mile and (4) four guns playing on and all the time the shells and solid shot flying all around us there was two killed and ten wounded in the regt but none in our company we captured one piece from them that was taken from us at shiloh we bivouacked on the battle ground that night without tents or blankets and it rained nearly all night the next day we took up our line of march and it commenced raining and we had one of the hardest rains that we have had this winter, nothing more transpired of note untill the thirtieth the 21st and 13th had quite a short fight and there was several killed and wounded and the next morning we had to go in to it we laid out that night within a hundred and fifty yards of the enemy no fire nor blankets so you can judge for your self how we slept the morning of the thirty first we were up in line at day light [there is another page and a half but it is so faint I can't read it. I did make out that it rained and lots of mud and that Rube was wounded in the right arm and hand.]

from your son
      Henry C Owen


Notes: He is referring to the Battle of Stones River, also known as Murfreesboro, that was Dec. 31–Jan. 2. Knob Gap, Tennessee, was part of the Battle at Stones River/ Murfreesboro.

******************************

Bethiah
                              Jan 29th 1863
   Dear Sister
                  I received your letter day before yesterday and was very glad to hear from you once more the pants came alright excellent thimbar [?] — I was not needing them at present we have drawn since I wrote before so that I am not suffering for clothes the socks came in — for I had but one pair and there was

no chance to get any more we are having very rainy weather here now [The next several lines are so faded I can't make them out. He does mention something about chicken and eggs and sitting around camp.] I would be very well if I could get it every week our duty is very heavy on us now there being so few men it is either go a foraging or on picket nearly every day so you see it keeps us tolerable busy we have only about twenty men for duty now I should like to be at home — and I am in hopes to be there before a great while my time is over half way anyhow so I have that much [several more lines that have faded so badly I can't make them out.] I should like very much to be there to go to school this winter for I think I could enjoy myself equally as well there as I can down here soldiering but I am here and expect to stay untill my time is out unless they make peace before but there is no use talking about that now for it don't help the matter at all I have stood the trip very well so far and think I can manage to get along some way untill my time is out no more at present give my respects to all enquiring friends and also tell — Clair that I have heard of a Reuben Reynolds

> From your Brother
> Henry Clarence Owen

Notes: Sorry I couldn't do any better on this one but it was barely visible.

*********************************

McLean Ills Feb 12 1863

Dear Father & Mother

Your letter of the 18th of January was received the 28th and you may be assured we were glad to hear from you and to hear you had received a letter from Clarence for I had watched the papers close by but could not see his name neither in the list of killed nor wounded so I supposed that he was either sick or had escaped unhurt, but still it did not satisfy us as it did to know for certain that he was well, I saw in the paper the death of Mr Lightfoot and any one can judge of what their Regiment had to do by reading the list of killed and wounded, Captain Alden was severely wounded and the commanding Officer of every other Company was killed, and it seems almost a miracle that Clarence escaped unhurt, but how much longer he will escape God only knows, and to think that while so many of our boys were suffering every thing and so many of them laying down their lives to put down this accursed rebellion that we should have so many Traitors (yes a hundred fold meaner than the Secesh) here at home who would be willing that every one of our noble boys should be killed rather than the Rebels should be conquered, it is too much. I sometimes wish our boys could be turned back and come home and mete out to the Scoundrels the justice they so richly deserve, I think we are having our share of the mud at any rate we are having a great deal more than is pleasant We received a letter from the East about a month ago containing the sad news of the death of Abby's Mother. She died the 6th of January and they wrote that it was quite sickly there this winter We are all usually well Abby & Eugene did not have the measles as for myself I hardly know whether I am better or not, I think I do not cough quite as much as I did in the fall but the weather has been so changing and I am most sure to take a little cold every time that it keeps me from gaining much. I am very weak I cannot even saw my wood and it is about as much as I can do to stay in the Store all day. I saw the Dr. the other day. he told me not to be discouraged that I need not expect to gain much such weather as we are having this winter. but he says I told you in the fall I could cure you and I am going to do it when it comes settled weather in the Spring but I am afraid it will be harder to do than he thinks for Abby was going to have written some too but I took a fix to write to day and she was busy and could not so you must excuse her this time. we send lots of love to all your affect.

Warren

Notes: This was in an envelope addressed to Jason Owen Esq Williamsville Sangamon County Ills. The postmark was McLean Ill, Feb 12. They didn't put years on their postmarks back then.

Warren was a half-brother of Clarence and Mary. The Mr. Lightfoot he refers to was Rube Lightfoot, mentioned in a number of Clarence's letters.

*******************************

Camp near Murfeesboro
March 28th 1863

Dear Sister

I received your letter to day and was very glad to hear from you there is not much of any thing going on here at present there has been some skirmishing here lately but every thing is quiet now our division has a great deal of scouting and picketing but that is nothing when a person gets used to it we have done so much of it that it don't seem natural for us to stay in camp I heard from John Lanterman the other day he was not expected to live the day out Mergenthaler is well We had a general review here the other day Old Rosy was around him self You seem to think an Oyster supper would be a great treat I have all I want to eat and all it costs me is the trouble of cooking them I have as good living here as I want biscuit butter ham fresh beef eggs potato and most every thing else that is good to eat.

I should like very much to visit your school but will have to wait untill some other time I must stop to get supper now Sunday evening supper is over I have a severe head ache and have had all the afternoon. I don't feel much like writing and think of nothing more at present tell mother that she need not send any more writing paper there is plenty here but I would like for you to send me two or three of Johnson & Bradfords 30s pens I received fathers letter about a week ago we was on picket then and have been on once since so you can guess for yourself what we have to do
write often from your Brother
Henry C O

Note: Old Rosy is General Rosecrans. He took over the Army of the Ohio/Cumberland.

\*\*\*\*\*\*\*\*\*\*\*\*\*\*\*\*\*\*\*\*\*\*\*\*\*\*\*\*\*\*\*\*

Camp near Murfresboro
April 27th 1863
Dear Sister
                    I received your letter a few days ago and I take this opportunity of answering it I am well at present
Because you expect to get married you must not think that every body else does I shall have no use for a wife after this war is over all I want will be a dog tent a sillet [skillet?] and a coffee pot and I can live just as well as I want to I got a letter from Warren two or three days ago they were all well then, times are very dull here there is not much stirring I was up town to day. there was three hundred prisoners brought in while I was there they are coming in nearly every day and a great many reffugees are coming in and giving

themselves up some of the prisoners that we have taken say that the rebels have but a few regiments that they can trust on out post duty for as sure as they get a chance they desert and come in to our lines and give themselves up I dont think of any thing more at present you must excuse bad writing for I could do no better with this pen and this kind of a place from your brother

H C Owen

*********************************

Sunday May 17th 1863

Dear Sister

I have this opportunity to answer your welcome letter that I received the 14th. The next day about 5 o clock in the afternoon to be ready to march immediately and several of the boys didn't even take any thing to eat and most all of us no blankets we went out four miles and stayed there two nights and this morning. we were relieved we could see the rebel pickets from where we were and some times our men change papers with them they were going to have a wedding today at the house where our cavalry videts stand and they gave our men an invitation to come if they wanted to

There is nothing new here at present the boys are arguing among them selves about what Genl. Hooker done and it would make you laugh to hear them talk [Part of the letter was cut off at this point so I will start where it starts again.] I got nothing for cooking fast day was observed here as far as it could Rosecrans is a religious man and allows no work to be done on sunday except what is actually necessary. I go to church when I can a good deal of the time we are on picket so that we can't go to church at all I don't think of any thing more at present

Write soon from your brother,

H. C. Owen

(PS) if you want my likeness I will have it taken and send it to you

Notes: The word videts should have been videttes. It also is spelled vedettes. A vedette is a mounted sentinel stationed in advance of pickets.

Genl. Hooker is Maj. Gen. Joseph "Fighting Joe" Hooker. Hooker had allowed his right flank to be rolled up by much superior Confederate soldiering under Stonewall Jackson at Chancellorsville.

*******************************

Camp near Winchester
Franklin. Co. Tenn

July 15th 1863

Dear Father

After much delay I take this opportunity of writing we came to this town the third of this month have a nice camp and good water and that is the main thing we are in sight of the Cumberland mountains one Brigade of Sheridans Division have been to Bridgeport I was out blackberrying to day this beats all places I ever saw there is a squad of thirty men goes out every day from our regiment and they fill their things every time this is the strongest secession hole in Tenn this county seceded long before the state some of the leading ones met in the court house and passed resolutions annexing the county to the state of Ala. I was on guard at Brigade Head Quarters and one guard stand at a house close and I was talking with the woman she said that she wished we would leave here that she was tired of us and wanted to know why we did not advance that Old Bragg was not here I told her that she need not be troubled for we had men enough after Bragg I suppose that you have heard all about what we did at Liberty gap the 2nd Ark. occupied a high hill covered with heavy timber and part of Johnstons men had been engaged with them nearly half a day and had been to the foot of the hill two or three times but were drove back each time their ammunition was exhausted then our regiment was ordered to charge the hill and we done it and drove the rebs and captured their flag when you go to Springfield just step into the State House and you can see it I had several trophies that I got on that hill but had to throw them away because I could not carry them Gen'l Johnston complimented us very highly for the manner in which we relieved his men it was but a very short time untill it was all over the whole army what a charge the 38th had made I think of nothing more at present Write soon from your son

Henry C Owen

(PS) please send some stamps


Notes: This was in an envelope addressed to Miss Mary Owen, Lincoln Logan Co Ills In care of Dr. Boston with a postmark of Nashville Ten Aug 8 1864 and a 3 cent stamp.

Winchester is south of Murfreesboro, Tennessee. Bridgeport is in Alabama. Liberty Gap is in Tennessee., between Bell Buckle, Tennessee, and Wartrace, Tennessee.

The 38th was involved in the Middle Tennessee or Tullahoma campaign Jun. 24–Jul. 7. They fought at Liberty Gap Jun. 24–27 and were part of the occupation of Middle Tennessee until Aug. 16.

# Chattanooga, Alabama, and Northwest Georgia

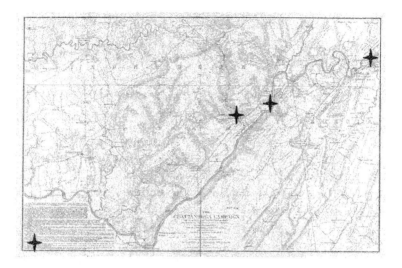

U.S. Army Corps of Engineers, *The Middle Tennessee and Chattanooga campaigns of June, July, August, and September 1863*, Map 4, J. von Glümer, New York: Julius Bien, 1891.

Highlighted Cities (southwest to northeast): Winston, Alabama, Stevenson, Alabama, Bridgeport, Alabama, Ooltewah, Tennessee

**Figure 6 — Chattanooga**

Stevenson, Ala
Aug 21st 1863

Dear Sister
     I take this opportunity to let you know of my whereabouts we are now at stevenson about thirty miles from winchester we got here yesterday about noon after three days hard marching over the mountains I have seen hills and rough roads but the road from here to winchester beats any thing I ever saw one of Genl Carlins orderlies was shot day before yesterday by a guerrilla he was back in the rear after the mail and the fellow was hid by the road and when the orderly came up he shot him in the side just above the hip bone but it is thought that he will get well Genl Sheridan has caught several bushwhackers since he has been here one of Genl Davises Orderlies was riding along on the mountain and one of these fellows shot at him but missed and the Orderly took after him and captured him and fetched him to camp he will be very apt to be hung the [not sure of these numbers but think it is 43] is here I am going to try to go and see them as soon as I can I have not seen them since we were at murfreesboro those stamps came through safe I dont think of any thing more now write soon from your brother

H C Owen

Notes: Col. Carlin was promoted to Brig. Gen. May 7, 1863.
    The 38th passed through the Cumberland Mountains, across the Tennessee River, and was involved in the Chickamauga, Georgia Campaign from Aug. 16–Sep. 22. The orderly that was shot was Joseph Hart.

\*\*\*\*\*\*\*\*\*\*\*\*\*\*\*\*\*\*\*\*\*\*\*\*\*\*\*\*\*\*\*\*

Sept 2nd 1863

Father

We are bivowacked for the night between the cumberland mountains and what is called the lookout mountains we crossed the river on Sunday about ten days march more and we will have the rebels at chatanooga cut off from all communication and if they are not careful we will take them in two companies of cavalry were out about two miles from here and caught two rebs one of them was a first sergeant three refugees came in to our lines and gave themselves up there several prisoners taken since we crossed the river it is the general opinion that we will have a hard fight at chatanooga but if we succeed in getting in the rear of them there will not be much fighting and it would suit us all much better not to have any fight I don't think of any thing more now I will write often and let you let you know what we are doing from your son

Henry C. Owen

Notes: The river he refers to crossing was the Tennessee River.

********************************

Winceton. Ala
Sept 5th 1863

Dear Sister

I have just received your letter of the 16th we have been on the move for some time but move very slow the roads are very rough and bad over the mountains yesterday our company were left to guard the bakery and did not get in camp untill 2 o clock this morning there is no signs of our moving yet to day still we are liable to move any time I don't

think of any thing more at present write soon from
your Brother

Henry C Owen

Notes:  Winceton is a misspelling for Winston, Alabama, which
is about 35 miles southwest of Chattanooga.

********************************

Dec 29, 1863

Dear Sister
I received your letter yesterday I
don't know as there is any thing to write tell mother
not to borrow any trouble on my account you will hear
of it soon enough when I get sick we are at Bridgeport
yet and will probably stay here this winter although
there has been some talk of our going to Knoxville a
day or two ago but I guess that has all died away at
least I hope so for we have good comfortable quarters
and plenty to eat and the latter is the main stay with a
soldier we had rather dull christmas I had a splendid
dinner better than the 114th I'll bet I have been on
picket once only since I came back you must not think
because we are down in dixie that we cant get any
thing night before last I was on picket and went out
about a mile from the picket to a frolic nothing more
this time write soon send me some stamps

Clarence

Notes:  Bridgeport is in Alabama. Since Clarence's last letter of
Sept. 5th, the 38th was involved in the Battle of Chickamauga Sep. 19–
20, 1863 and the siege of Chattanooga, Sept. 24–Oct. 27, 1863. The
reopening of the Tennessee River occurred Oct 26–29. The 38th then

moved to Bridgeport, Alabama, where they remained until Jan. 26, 1864. However, in this letter, he mentions "since I came back" so I am wondering if he went home or on sick leave and perhaps missed these battles. In Nov., the 38th was attached to the 1st Brigade, 1st Division, 4th Army Corps until Jun. 1865. Rosecrans was replaced by Thomas and then Grant. Carlin was given a new command in Nov.

\*\*\*\*\*\*\*\*\*\*\*\*\*\*\*\*\*\*\*\*\*\*\*\*\*\*\*\*\*\*\*\*\*\*

Jan 30th 1864

Dear Sister
         We did not march to day so I take this opportunity to answer your letter I received the socks and mittens the day before we left Bridgeport but did not get the letter for three days afterward have orders to prepare for a campaign immediately our destination is unknown but supposed to be Knoxville the rebels are concentrating their forces there we are now about twelve miles south east of Chat Bridgeport is in Ala no more this time write soon direct to Knoxville I will write again the next opportunity

         Clarence

26th.         Notes: The 38th moved to Ooltewah, Tennessee, beginning Jan.

\*\*\*\*\*\*\*\*\*\*\*\*\*\*\*\*\*\*\*\*\*\*\*\*\*\*\*\*\*\*\*\*\*

Camp 38th Ills
Ooltawah, Tenn

February 22nd 1864

Dear Sister
                    I received your letter last night and was
glad to hear from you once more we have been having
some very cold weather lately but is quite warm to day
was out on a scout last week started wednesday night
marched all night and the next day and captured
twelve Prisoners was within thirteen miles of Dalton I
believe that I never was tired in my life as when we got
back to camp we have been here almost two weeks
and there is some prospect of our staying some time
have had a splendid time since we have been here last
week there was a Party nearly every night we are now
in what is called east Tenn and of course there is
several Union Ladies here that makes the time pass
more pleasantly it is nothing uncommon to see the
stars & stripes in front of a house here something that
we have not been used to for over two years
Imagine Yourself sitting in a shelter Tent holding a
book with one hand and writing on it with the other
then you can see how I look at present the rumors you
have heard in regard to this Regiment reenlisting are
false there was considerable excitement for a while it
has all died away now and there has about twenty
enlisted our company put their names down to go
providing the Regiment went but they failed to get the
Regiment in so we burnt the paper tell Theodore that I
say for him not to enlist untill I come back or at least
untill he hears from me again and tell Jimmy Post
that if he is not sworn in he better take a fools advice
and not go at present tell him that if he wants to know
why to write and I will tell him but the best thing is to

stay where he is at present I think of nothing more now give my respects to all the folks tell Hulda that I should be very glad to hear from her my greatest enjoyment here is reading letters from home Write soon

Your Brother
Clarence

Notes: This letter was mailed from Chattanooga, Tennessee, Feb. 28th, 1864 and was addressed to Jason Owen, Elkhart Logan Co. Ill.
Dalton is in Georgia. The 38th regiment re-enlisted Feb. 29, 1864. Veterans were placed on furlough Mar. 28 to Jun. 9, rejoining the regiment at Ackworth, Georgia. Non-veterans were attached to the 101st Ohio Infantry during this time.

\*\*\*\*\*\*\*\*\*\*\*\*\*\*\*\*\*\*\*\*\*\*\*\*\*\*\*\*\*\*\*\*

Camp 38 Ills
Ooltawah Tenn
February 27th 1864
Dear Father
As I wrote to the Girls two or three days ago I have not much news now they got up considerable excitement last night on the Veteran cause and there is some prospect of the regiment going if they do I shall go with them and if Horatio has not come home I would like to have him wait untill we find out whether or not the Regiment goes if it does we will be there by the first of April at the L—tsid [latest?] and should be very glad to see him no more this time from your son

Clarence

Notes: This is in an envelope addressed to Jason Owen Esq, Elkhart Logan County Illinois with a postmark of Ea—ville N.Y. May 21 and a 3 cent stamp. There are two other letters in the same envelope.

55

# Reenlistment Break

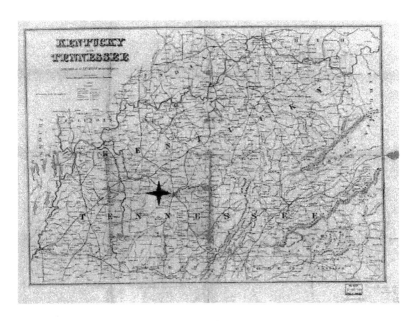

O. Lederle, *Kentucky and Tennessee*, O. Lederle Litho., 1862.

Highlighted City: Nashville

**Figure 7 — Tennessee**

Nashville
May 21st 1864

Dear Sister

I have nothing to do at present so
I will write you a few lines have been here since
yesterday morning expect to leave for Chattanooga
this afternoon at four O clock but don't know whether
or not we will get away I saw Mergenthaler yesterday
he is well I had a dish of ripe strawberries yesterday
don't you wish you were down in Dixie we have some
of the nicest Bouquets here you ever see but we are
getting quite tired of this Place want to get down to the
front where we can breathe pure air and have some
liberties again we have had a very pleasant time while
traveling but as soon as we stopped they put us in
Baracks and the Officers would run off and leave us
and it took hard work to get out I have not been in the
Baracks here since we came here yesterday morning
nothing more write soon direct to Chattanooga love to
all

Clarence


Notes: In different hand writing, on the back of the letter, it
says Elkhart August 15th 1864, Elb.

# The Siege of Atlanta

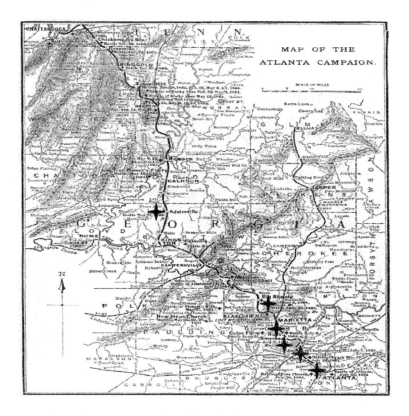

*Map of the Atlanta campaign. [May-Sept. 1864]*, 1887

Highlighted Places (northwest to southeast):  Adairsville, Big Shanty, Marietta, Ruff's Station, Chattahoochee River, Atlanta

**Figure 8 — Georgia**

Adairsville Ga.

June 4th 1864

Dear Sister

Three weeks ago today I left home
for the last time now we are within ten miles of
Kingston leave here at five o clock in the morning for
that Place We left —att—oon Sunday night and
Monday afternoon we were in Louisville stayed there
three days then went to Nashville stayed over night
and day then started for Chattanooga but came very
near not getting there. the Rebels put a Torpedo in the
road four miles this side of Tulahoma and it would
have blown part of our Regt sky high if a Horse had
come along before the train and run against the string
that was fixed to explode the Torpedo but as it was the
were only thrown off the track and two men badly hurt
there were more hurt slightly this was about three o
clock in the morning and we got the train on to the
track all but three cars ready to start by ten o clock
short day got into about three o clock the next
morning stayed there nearly a week started from there
just a week ago to day with a drive of cattle I expect
tomorrow will bring our journey to an end for a while I
left the Regt monday morning at Ringgold took the
cars for Resaca got a turn their went to Chattanooga
fifty miles just two by our selves and back again
overtook the Regt last night about three miles this side
of Resaca set up our Ranch got Breakfast at five then
packed up and come to this Place fourteen miles
cooked Dinner and Supper have to be ready to march
at five in the morning we will get to Kingston by noon I
had one of the nicest little Ponies you ever see but
traded him off today if my time had been nearly out I
would kept him and brought him home with me may
be I will happen on to another sometime this fellow
was a perfect picture I hated to let him go but had

wery of keeping him safe we have not had any mail at all yet but expect to get some at Kingston when we get there it is getting late so I will stop untill tomorrow

Sunday evening June 5th

We marched only about eight miles went out forageing this afternoon we are about two miles and three quarters from Kingston have my Ranch in a House the Folks here have been very rich very large Plantation fine House now they have not got anything to eat they are all nearly starved I have been feeding them since we came here there is only twenty four of them I don't think of anything more at present write soon love to all

Your Brother
Clarence

Notes: Resaca and Kingston are in Georgia. Ringgold is also in the western part of Georgia. Tullahoma is in Tennessee.

The Atlanta campaign began in May 1864 and lasted into Sept. The 38th was at Tunnel Hill from May 6 – 7. They next fought in the Battle at Rocky Faced Ridge from May 8–13, including Buzzard's Roost Gap from May 8–9, and a demonstration on Dalton, Georgia from May 9–13. They proceeded to the Battle of Resaca from May 14–15. They were near Kingston from May 18–19, near Cassville on May 19 and advanced on Dallas, Georgia, from May 22–25. They were involved in operations on the line of Pumpkin Vine Creek and battles about Dallas, New Hope Church and Allatoona Hills from May 25–Jun. 5.

********************************

Big Shanty Ga
June 17th 1864

Dear Sister

I received your long looked for letter yesterday afternoon and I need not tell you that I was glad to hear from home once more I had almost made up my mind that you were never going to write

61

was out on the line when I received your letter have
been fighting for this the sixth day now and have
drove them nearly four miles the Rebs fell back over a
mile last night or rather this morning before day light
our skirmishers were in their breast works at day light
we joined the Brigade on the ninth of this month
belong to the 1st Brig 1st Division 4th Corps but on to
Pat Clyburnes Division whipping us that is a mistake
for we have drove him nearly four miles in the last
week that is the way he has whipped us a Captain on
Gen'l Howards staff said this morning that we would
establish head Qt's in Marietta to but I have my
doubts about that but think we will be there before
three days I was close enough this morning to see the
College I had an opportunity yesterday of seeing what
I have wanted to see for a long time that is an Artillery
Drill and yesterday afternoon I was upon the top of a
high hill where I could see the whole length of our
lines also the Rebs too could see where every one of
the shells bursted strawberries have been gone for
some time but we have other Fruit to fill their place
Cherries mulberries and Whortle berries are ripe and
black Berries will be in a few days so you see that we
are a head of you in some respects if we cant have P—
enies we can make fight with the Rebs and that will
answer every purpose you never told me whose
photograph you had got I saw the 64th the other day
the Boys were all well except John Lindsay he had
quite unwell for several days but had managed to keep
up with the Regt met with George Beck yesterday
afternoon he was unwell but I think he will get over it
soon his time is out to day and I think that is enough
to cure any person at least it would me I don't care
how sick I was I don't think of any thing more now
love to all write soon tell Hulda that she must not wait
for me to write for it is very little time we get to write

now with regards and best wishes I remain Your
Brother

Clarence

Notes: This was also in the same envelope as the Feb 27th 1864
letter.

A whortle berry is a blueberry. Pat Clyburne is actually General
Pat Cleburne. Marietta is in Georgia, just outside of Atlanta. The 38th was
involved in operations around Marietta and against Kennesaw Mountain
from Jun. 10–Jul. 2. They fought at Pine Hill from Jun. 11–14 and Lost
Mountain from Jun. 15–17.

\*\*\*\*\*\*\*\*\*\*\*\*\*\*\*\*\*\*\*\*\*\*\*\*\*\*\*\*\*\*\*\*

Before Marietta Ga.
Tuesday June 28th 1864

Dear Sister
I received your letter this
afternoon and need not tell you that I was glad to hear
from home once more had been looking for several
days and finally give up getting any word soon You
must not wait for me to write but write as often as you
can tell Hulda that I should like to hear from her.
I hardly know what to write perhaps you would
like to know what we are doing down here well I will
give you a brief sketch we are having a long hard
campaign joined the command on the nineth of this
month have been in the front ever since and every
thing bids fair at present for us to spend the fourth of
July on the skirmish line have drove the rebels back
from one line of marks after another untill we have got
them to their last ditch nearly we made a charge on
their works yesterday and was repulsed but was
successful on our right and left our loss was very
heavy there is some move on foot tonight but what it

is I cant tell we are ordered to be ready to march at a moments warning with ten days rations the first two weeks it rained nearly every day but we have had no rain for a week now still it has the appearance of rain at present.

I should be very glad to be at your picnic it would much more preferable than being picked out by the Rebels as we are down here but never mind this cruel war is not going to last always our turn to go to picnics and parties will come after a while then we will enjoy it so much the better

I am thinking that I will have to give you a lecture about writing You leave out some words some you join together so that it is hard to tell what they are perhaps you will think that I had better look at home a little about writing I received fathers letter two or three days stating that he had sent the money I have sent to Chattanooga for it but have not heard whether it has come or not. Tell Sue that I supposed she wanted her Photograph or she would not have asked me for it so I sent it to her and as matter of course I suggested mine nothing more at present write soon love to all with regards and best wishes I remain Your Brother Clarence

PS Our Brigade made a charge on the 22nd of this month and George Beck was wounded through both legs and had to have his left leg taken off and died the next day but one after you can tell his Sister the first chance you have for she will be anxious to hear from him

Clarence
Wednesday 29th
had  quite a fight last night after I stopped writing this morning the firing was all stopped and I went out on the skirmish line and could see the Johnny Rebs in

their works their line of works and ours is not over
two hundred yards apart changed papers with them
this forenoon we can get Rebel Papers of later date
than we can our own we have plenty of music here but
very from the music that you have up there. nothing
more        Clarence


Notes:  The 38th assaulted Kennesaw Jun. 27.

\*\*\*\*\*\*\*\*\*\*\*\*\*\*\*\*\*\*\*\*\*\*\*\*\*\*\*\*\*\*\*\*\*\*

Near N— Dow Ga
July 4th 1864

Father
        I received the money Saturday all safe
Our sutler was up Chattanooga last week and I sent
an order by him for it I have not time to write much
now this fourth was spent fighting all day was out on
the skirmish line this afternoon came in just before
dark the Johnnies left Marietta yesterday morning
about three O clock probably the next time you hear
from me we will be in Atlanta nothing more this time
write soon

        Clarence


Notes:  This was in the same envelope as the Feb. 27th 1864
letter. Starting about this time his hand writing got a lot worse and looked
very hurried.
        A sutler is a civilian provisioner to an army post. He also can be
the camp cook.
        The 38th was at Ruff's Station, Georgia, on Jul. 4.

\*\*\*\*\*\*\*\*\*\*\*\*\*\*\*\*\*\*\*\*\*\*\*\*\*\*\*\*\*\*\*\*

Chatahoochie River
July 11th, 1864

Dear Mother
I received Your welcome letter
yesterday am well at present have been quite unwell
but not so but what I kept along am getting along with
the Ranch fine. this has been the longest Campaign
that we have ever had and I hardly think it is over yet
just one month ago day before yesterday we joined the
Brig out Achworth and since that time have been
skirmishing nearly every day where we were yesterday
morning we could see Atlanta and all the Rebells
works and their Army but have moved to the left now
part of the Army has crossed the River already and we
expect to cross soon still we may stay where we are for
a few days received orders to day to clean up camp
but we won't stay more than a week although I
suppose it will depend altogether upon the movements
of the "Johnnies" we can take Atlanta most any time it
may take several days but take it we will when we
start for it You spoke in your last about Clybornes
Division having a fight with Stanleys and whipping
them but that is false for we belong to Stanleys
Division and have been in front of "Pat" Clyborne all
the time at Dalton Clybornes Division numbered seven
thousand now they number three thousand three
hundred and they have never driven us an inch that is
the way they have whipped Stanley.

I have met "crazy Bill" Genl Sherman several times in the last month he is a very common looking man if it was not for his uniform you would sooner take him for an old Farmer than any thing else. he does not look any thing like the picture the Girls have I must stop now but will write more when we get to Atlanta from

Your Son<br>Clarence

Notes:    This was in an envelope addressed to Miss Mary E. Owen, Williamsville Sangamon Co Ills with a 3 cent stamp. On the envelope is a US Flag with "Liberty and Union now, and forever, one and inseparable." written under the flag. In the same envelope was a 2nd letter dated April 6, 1862.

The 38$^{th}$ was at Chattahoochie River from Jul. 5–17.

********************************

In front of Atlanta<br>August 3$^{rd}$ 1864

Dear Sister

I received Your welcome letter day before yesterday and as the mail goes out this afternoon thought I would write a few lines we have not got Atlanta yet but have been in sight of it nearly two weeks You no doubt have heard before this of the fight on the 20 & 22 I sent a paper home a few days ago that tells what the 4 Corps has done since we came here. as soon as I can I will send an Official report of the fight that will be reliable.

I suppose that when I come home again You will favor me with some music on the Piano and I am in hopes that will not be long. We can whip the whole

southern Confederacy by detail if they will bring them
here to Us I have nothing more to write now
With regards and best wishes
I remain Your Brother
Clarence

Notes:   The Battle of Atlanta lasted from Jul. through Sept.
1864. The 38th fought at Peach Tree Creek from Jul. 19–20 and in the
siege of Atlanta from Jul. 22–Aug. 25.

\*\*\*\*\*\*\*\*\*\*\*\*\*\*\*\*\*\*\*\*\*\*\*\*\*\*\*\*\*\*\*\*\*\*

Normal Aug 17th 1864
Dearly Loved Parents
I can scarcely control my
feelings to write you Oh! what a sunden shock, it
seemed for the moment my heart would burst, the
next moment I could not realize that he was gone from
us, never more to return Oh can it so? Yes it so, how
lonely everything seems, It seems as if I could not
remain another hour here; but hasten to you & our
lonely home, where no more we shall hear his voice, or
see his form again. No loving Mother or Sisters were
near to smooth his forehead, or hear his dying words;
no kind friends were near, to lay his body in its last
resting place. He died a noble death & it will be only a
short time, ere we shall meet him in that land of
brightness.

The teachers are returning from the institute,
this long afternoon has at last nearly passed, the sun
is about sinking in the west, ere another sunset others
may be grieving for those that have lain down their
lives for their country What a glorious thought he has
given his all to his country without a murmer
Thursday noon, I have been up to the institute; but I
can not remain, it seems as if it would crush me I

shall start for home to day & reach Elkhart Saturday
Good by till then   Your daughter Bithia


Notes: On the next page of the same letter starts this next letter.


*********************************


Normal, Aug 18. 1864.
Dear Friends
             I take my pen hardly knowing
what to say to you on this sad and unlooked for
occasion. what sudden news, and so unexpected. was
it unexpected to us, because Clarence had been
preserved through so many severe fights! because the
blows had been warded off, as by a kind Providential
hand! Amid your sorrows, it truly is a consolation to
you to know that this earth is not our only home, to
feel that there is a brighter world <u>above</u>.
      I feel that I can sympathize with you in your
sad bereavement The morning before we read of the
death of Clarence I wrote a line to the friends at home,
in commemoration of the burial of our youngest
Sister. I well recollect the <u>sadness</u> of my heart, at that
time, the pleasures of the world were robbed of their
charms and I felt that there was gloom on everything
around. But when I looked above there was hope. We
will go to our friends though they will never return to
us.
      B.'s is so overcome with the trial that she
cannot go into society Perhaps it would be better for
her to remain here, but I cannot say to her "forget
your sorrow. be cheerful." my heart speakings would
not allow it.

Good Bye dear friends and may God sustain
you in this sad bereavement.

From your affectionate

Hulda


Notes: This was in an envelope address to Jason Owen Esq. Elk
Hart Ill. with a postmark of Normal Ill Aug.

These last two letters came as a shock to us as we read them. Of
course, we knew that Clarence had been long dead, but did not know of
him until we read these letters. We became so engrossed in his life, that it
was as if a close family member had just died, rather than something that
happened more than 150 years ago.

Clarence was killed on Aug. 6, 1864 during the Siege of
Atlanta. He was twenty years old at the time, on his second tour with the
38th Regiment, having served for just over three years. The marker in the
Elkhart Cemetery is a memorial marker. He is buried, along with many
of his fellow soldiers, in the Marietta National Cemetery in Marietta,
Georgia.

There is nothing to indicate that he served with particular
distinction, nor even any direct evidence that he killed or wounded
anyone. There is also nothing to indicate that his service was less than
honorable. His only mentions in the daily rolls were that he was fined $3
in a general court-martial, no particulars were given, and that he was
AWOL in Sept. of 1863. He was listed as AWOL following a major
battle, and did not return for two weeks. As there was no disciplinary
action taken, the previously mentioned court-martial was held prior to
this incident, we assume he just became separated from his Company
during the fighting and had trouble finding them after the battle. This was
not an uncommon occurrence.

He was just an average soldier, doing his best, day in and day
out, but as the best military leaders will tell you, that makes him more
deserving of respect and admiration than the finest of Generals.

# Chapter 3 — After the War

The Next three letters are from Mary Elizabeth Ross Leach. She was the wife of Adoniram Judson Leach, who was the brother of Abigail Leach Owen. Adoniram died in 1865.

*********************************

Eaton Sept 15 [no year]

My Dear Sister

An Apology is due from me to you and I humbly confess my negligence although it was unintionall you will be surprised to learn that after A was Buried my Son in Conn wrote for me to come there and get rested as he had been here while A was sick and knew how worn I was from Sleepless Nights and anxious care for I assure you I never Dreamed he would have to Suffer so long and bear it as well and Patient as he did had suppose his disease was of that Nature he would Easily and gradually go down I had watched him so long for fear he would drop away and I not be near that I could not sleep even after he had ceased to need our care my Friends thought the best thing for me to do was to go and take Minnie with me for she was called to Bury A Sister the Tuesday after A was buried I could not do better so in just two weeks I Packed and went I started the 14th of August and returned home last Evening the 14 of Sept I ought to have wrote you again after the Funeral and did intend to but was waiting to hear from you and left word if any letters came to me from you to send them to Howard and thought they would, any them to you Howard was in last evening said they did not get any sent to me but had one to them if your letter is lost it is the first I received your Postal after my arrival hear last Night, I am rested some but, O to come home to this lonesome House made so by Death you must know how very lonesome we must be to come home after shutting the house up so long but I must bear it and hope I may have grace to wait till my time should come to bid adieu to dear ones on Earth and gain those that have gone before you and Daniel here probably received the Notice to prove the Will you may be anxious as it is Natural that you should wish to know if your Brother left you any thing I am happy to inform you he did $500 and after the Legacy have been paid that he mentioned the remainder is to be divided equally between the two Brothers Da H A wished me to give you the Life of Dr. Rendrick if you have not got it do you want it sent by Mail or wait an opportunity A had just got A new Jones Truss did not wear it but one day it is A Double Truss and if I thought Daniel could wear it I would send it to him please ask him and remember me to all my Friends there and write often and ever think of me as your own dear Sister Mary

my heart is drawn closer than ever to the Brothers and Sisters of my Dear Husband and may the Lord forbid that any thing should separate or come between us in any way yours in Affliction
M H Leach

Notes: A is Mary's deceased husband, Adoniram. The two brothers Mary refers to are DA, who is Daniel Standish Leach, and H, who is Henry Howard Leach. I believe this was written in 1865, the year Adoniran died.

\*\*\*\*\*\*\*\*\*\*\*\*\*\*\*\*\*\*\*\*\*\*\*\*\*\*\*\*\*\*\*\*

Janury 21th 1866

Brother and Sister Owen

I was glad to hear
from you in a letter I received last Tusday that you are
well and injoy your selves so well and have so many
friends,

The sad trial of the sale is over and Oh how's it
made my poor heart ache to see horses and cattl leave
the home that Adonoran love to feed and tend so well,
it seems like opening afreash the wound that will
never heal

I kept John and Dol 4 cows part of the sheep,
gray colt and all the stock hogs, the sale was well
attended some two hundred or more was here things
went pretty well on an average some high and some
low. the cattle went the best I got over 8 cts for the
fattening hogs   Brother Wm is still with me I do not
know what I should have done if he had not come he
is like a Father to me, more then a brother, he is
agoing to build for me if he has time, they comence
tomorrow to draw brick while the roads are good I
have Edger Brown (a Nephew of Roslindas) staying
with me now John Hensler has left, he drank to much
I could not get along with him I have another hand by
the name of Moor, Danal was over to day they are all
well, Ida went to Huldas Saturday morning to meet
Berthia they are well, You wrote that Horance was
coming Ida is looking her eyes out for him
Milie is quite well, is getting harty and full of mischief
a great pet of his Uncol Will

Do you remember the picture that hangs over
the bed it is a certificate for the Missionary Society
with a picture of our savour arising from the tomb,
ever since Adonorans death he calls the picture of our
savour his Pa the first weeks after his death every one
most that came in he would pull them to the bed and

say see see, pa, pa, and now when I aske him where
Pa is he points to it is it not remarkible?
We have very cold weather now Mrs Peter Lanterman
does not have good health Baby Lightfoot is quite sick
Jackson has not left yet Their is a great many after
land, do you want some Berthia said you did I rented
80 acres last evening
Tell Mary Austin I received her letter with thanks and
will answer when I hear of her returning from NY am
sorry to hear of Gustains bad health, write soon,
remember me to all the friends and love to you from
your

aflicted sister
Mary H R Leach

22th
PS we can get along untill you make your visit out.
Berthia will be over again in 2 weekes she had got a
letter from Mary she was well, snowing now


Notes:    This was on stationery rimmed in black and in an
envelope addressed to Mr Jason Owen Eaton Madison Co N.Y with a
postmark of Elkhart City Ill Jan. The envelope is also trimmed in black.
       Berthia and Ida are the daughters of Henry Howard Leach.
Rosalinda was the wife of Henry Howard Leach.

*******************************

Eaton Feb 9th [no year was given]

My Dear Sister
              I am reminded in reading yours that I am
in debt to you for your last letter which found us all
well as usual so are Howard and Family the weather
for the past week has been very stormy since Feb we
have considerable snow and the prospect for more A
remarkable winter here but favorable for many Poor
who have not the comforts of Life how thankful we

ought to be that god has Blessed us thus far provided for our wants

We have been very busy this Winter in getting Minnie ready for Housekeeping the first of March I believe I wrote she was to go upon the Maurton Farm is to Marry Charles Morton will send you A Card of invitation in this and as you open this you will recognize the Profile A has kept so long thinking you will prize it more then anyone else I send it to you Harriet says it is A true Profile of your Mother

Charles and Family have moved in with us he is building A small Shop to Bottle Beer he thinks he will make it pay well

Ida and Rosalinda was here week before last is looking well and seems happy in her home Berdeth talks some of coming home to work the Farm as the two youngest Boys are going in to A Cheese Factory I don't know yet where Horatio is going

Perhaps you hear from them there is some Changes in Eaton Mrs Hunt died two weeks ago Mrs Elsa Campbel is moving into the House Mrs George Ellis built Mr Hunt Bought it and had just got settled as he died 2 years ago Mrs H had sold and was going back into her old House with her Brother Hirem but the Lord took her to her Heavenly home so we are passing rapidly away and in A little it will be said of us we are Dead are we ready is my work done I ask myself what am I doing for the cause which ought to lie nearest my Heart I hope to do every duty made known Minnie rec A letter from Huldah A short time ago am glad she is doing well and also that Mary is trying to do what is right and may she be kept by the Power of God through Faith unto Salvation is my Prayer as well as the rest remember me to Henrietta with all the rest and write often yours Affectionately

Mary H Leach

Notes:    Rosalinda was Henry Howard's wife and Ida and Berdeth, also previously referred to as Berthia, were their daughters. Although no year was given on this letter, I believe it was written in 1866. Mary is writing to Abigail Leach Owen, her sister-in-law.

# Chapter 4 — Mary Owen from Golconda

Warner, Higgins & Beers, et al. *Atlas of Kendall Co. and the state of Illinois: to which is added an atlas of the United States*, 1870. p. 23.

Highlighted Cities (south to north): Golconda, Elkhart, Normal

**Figure 9 — Illinois**

Mary was the youngest of the Owen children. She was born in 1849. Though only fifteen at the time of his death, she corresponded with Clarence, being one of the sisters to which he referred in the letters. We do not have any of her letters to Clarence during that time.

In 1869, at the age of twenty, Mary left home in Elkhart to teach in Golconda, Illinois. Golconda is near the southern tip of the state, on the Ohio River. It is more than 200 miles from Elkhart, which is in the center of the state, near Springfield. This was a considerable trip at that time.

It is not certain where "Mate" as she was sometimes called by friends and family, taught. She only refers to it in the letters as "The Institute." We also don't know what subject or subjects, or the level that she taught, though from the spelling, grammar, and punctuation in her letters, I am guessing she did not teach English. I hope you enjoy learning about the life of a young woman on her own, just after the Civil War, as much as we did.

*********************************

Golconda Sunday Sept 7 1869

My Dear Parents

Just one week ago I arrived in Golconda We were met at the landing by a delegation of directors and scholars and escorted to the hotel. Such a reception as we had! Newcomb and Alice were almost devoured by the people. We found the directors in a great deal of trouble. They could not find a boarding place for us. It seems to me help is more scarce here than at home even. You would have thought to see them work, that it was their own family they were trying to find boarding for. finally in desperation one of the directors said if I would put up with the room he would take me and Newcomb and Alice could take day board. They have succeeded in getting a very pleasant room in the next house and I am settled in the Sweat Box for that is what they call my room on account of its being so warm. Mr and Mrs

McCoy the people we board with are very pleasant.
Mrs McCoy is from  —P—cout [it looks like YePrucout]
When I say they are very kind I only say for
them what I can say of every one I have come in
contact with.
The institute commenced a week ago yesterday
and lasted till three days
Of course we all had to go to the Institute.
Newcomb was the biggest gun there. They think down
here there never was such a man.
Friday I went to a Sabbath school convention
about 4 miles out in the country. over stories up hills
a quarter of a mile long through the woods and over
stumps we went. I would rather go eight miles at
home.
Sat. Well I commenced this Tuesday. Every
night since then we have had company or have been
out. Last night we attended a party. Had a very
pleasant time.
I am going to say a few words about my school
before I forget it. I have 57 names aged from 6 to 9.
may be half a dozen 12 years old.
Of course I am just as busy as I can be from 9
AM till 4 ½ PM and so far there has been a good deal
to do evenings. I think after we get fairly started we
shall have less to do evenings.
I am going to do the best I can in this school.
Newcomb and Alice are both so good to me.
If I have not said anything of the scenery here it
isn't because I haven't thought of it. It is a picture to
me all of the time. The Ohio rivers right before our
house. To the right and back of us the ground rises
almost perpendicularly. This is known as "Co's hill".
On the top of the hill overlooking both river and town
is a little old brick house that looks as if it were build
centuries ago. An old man, a German, a son of a

nobleman lives here. The grounds are beautiful trees
flower walks, rusticosen to are everywhere and over all
their is such quaint look. It looks as I always imagined
a scene on the Rhine might look.
Why do you not write? Of course you have
received my letter written at Cairo.
I have been from home two weeks and not one word.
Love to all of the friends and do please write often.
Now goodbye
Your daughter down in Egypt.


Notes: Egypt is an area of southern Illinois from about level
with St. Louis, down to the southern tip at Cairo. It is cut off to the east
by the Wabash River, to the south by the Ohio River, and to the west by
the Mississippi River. Golconda is in the southeastern portion of
"Egypt."

\*\*\*\*\*\*\*\*\*\*\*\*\*\*\*\*\*\*\*\*\*\*\*\*\*\*\*\*\*\*\*

Golconda. Sept. 26. 1869.
My Dear Parents.
I received your very
welcome letters last Thursday and as I was just
sending a letter to Bertha and Frank, I directed it to
you at Elkhart. I think it is very strange that you have
not heard from me. I have kept writing and wondering
why you didn't answer. I thought you would write any
way whether you heard from me or not.
I presume this irregularity in the mail is owing
partly to the steamboats. Since I came down here
there have been two boats blown up within a few miles
of Golconda.
I was so sorry to hear you were having such a
time with chills up there, and Frank too. I hope he is
much better. I think he has been working too hard.

As for me, dont worry about my getting sick for I'm not going to indulge in any such luxury. I have to work very hard and get very tired but I like it very much here. If I could only see my old Father and Mother once a week I should be happy.

Now have you all enjoyed the fruit I have eaten for you. If you enjoyed it half as much as I did I am satisfied.

I have almost lived on fruit. The children bring us bushels of peaches pears plums apples quinces pawpaws etc. Oh I assure you Egypt is a great place.

It seems very sad to hear Mr. Yancleve is so much worse. I am afraid Grace will have to come back alone.

And Emma is home sick. tell her she ought to be ashamed right there among friends. I'm not going to be home sick at all. Newcomb and Alice are just as good to me as they can be. and it just so with everybody here. I cant help being pleased and contented. Being a missionary to the heathen isnt so bad after all.

I'm only going to write a short letter this time. I want you to write every week whether you hear from me or not and I'll do the same then we cant help getting letters some time.

Give my love to Aunt Mary and tell her I am going to write in a few days. Love to Mrs Shreve and all the rest of the friends.

Now do either one or both of you write me once a week.

I do feel so disappointed when the mail comes day after day and nothing for me.

And now good night and <u>heaps</u> of love from Your daughter

Mary

I forgot to say I have 79 pupils
My compliments to Jack. Is he as affectionate
as ever?


Notes: This was in an envelope addressed to Jason Owen Esq.
Elkhart Logan Co. Illinois. The postmark is Golconda Ill Nov.
Bertha is Mary's sister. Bertha married Benjamin Franklin
(Frank) Bice.

\*\*\*\*\*\*\*\*\*\*\*\*\*\*\*\*\*\*\*\*\*\*\*\*\*\*\*\*\*\*\*\*

Golconda Oct 31 1869
My Dear Father & Mother.
                    I finished a letter to
you last Friday night mailed it yesterday I suppose
you will get it in about a week I declare it is awful
provoking the times we have about getting letters. I
have received your last letter containing the check The
letter reached here just eight days after it was mailed
    I presume you will want to know first, how I am
feeling Much better than when I wrote last. I have not
had any chills since I commenced this new medicine.
If the chills will only let me alone until I get over being
so weak and nervous I shall be so glad. When I wrote
last week I felt utterly discouraged and worn out.
There is one thing though for which I am very
thankful. I am in good hands
    Mrs McCoy is one of the kindest and best of
nurses. I don't know of but one person that is better
and that is you, Ma.
    You asked what I paid for board. I don't know
yet. Everything is furnished now.
Our washing, the way we do now we hire our washing
and ironing separate. We pay a woman one dollar to
come and do the washing, no matter how much or

how little. I pay one third of this. Then for the ironing we pay twenty-five cents per day. This we find costs us on the average only a little over half as much as it did to pay in the usual way, one dollar a dozen.

Ma you remember about Mrs Goodsell promising to crochet Sarah a tidy [a receptacle for holding small items]. She hasn't done it and Im going to make her one for a Christmas present if I can get it done. You know there is a good deal of work in one and I have very little time, but it is work I can take up any time.

About the dress I thought of getting, I thought I would like a plaid alapaca [alpaca?]. The cost will be about the same as a good black. I wrote to Sarah, asking her what she thought about it. The hat I cant tell what it would cost. I supose may be a bare hat might be got for $1.00 or $1.50. I should think it ought to, then if I had a plume a good one could not be got for less than $4.00. I had rather not have any unless I do get a good one. I have tried cheap ones enough to know they are the dearest in the end. I think I shall have to send to Sarah to get the things for there is no chance what ever to get any thing here Every thing is double price and no first quality of dress goods are brought on. They don't know what a good price of alapaca is. Ma I wish I had my merino here. I can make a dress as pretty as new of it. You may smile but I can. Alice has one, I should make an over skirt of something else. I wish you would see what it would cost to express it to me.

You wanted to know what I thought about your getting a suit. I think it would be nice, and believe I would get it. I wish you would send me two or three of those trix types [don't know this] the next time you write. I received a letter from Bertha the same night yours came. Shall answer in a day or two.

There was something I wanted to ask you about but
cant think what now.

I am glad you didn't mean to scold me. your letter
made me feel real blue.

I don't remember what I wrote. in fact I don't
remember writing anything about any gentleman. I
suppose it was some ridiculous nonsense that
happened to come in my head at the time and never
gave another thought. And now good bye and lots of
love. Mary

Notes: This was in an envelope addressed to Jason Owen Esq.
Elkhart Illinois but with a postmark of Sept 29 Golconda Ill.

We have been trying to figure out who Sarah is. The best we
have come up with is a girl named Sarah Camel, who was born in 1838,
and was listed as living with the Jason Owen family in the 1850 census.
The Owen and Camel families were close and we are guessing her
parents may have died and she came to live with the Owens. In later
letters she is linked with James, whom we believe she married. But we
haven't been able to confirm any of this.

\*\*\*\*\*\*\*\*\*\*\*\*\*\*\*\*\*\*\*\*\*\*\*\*\*\*\*\*\*\*\*\*\*\*

Golconda, November. 10. 1869.

My Dear Parents.

Your welcome letter was
received last Friday night. I sent a letter to you
Monday, but as it was one I had written before I
received your letter I thought I would write again
tonight.

I have 93 scholars now. Pretty good sized
school, Isn't it?

I havent had but two chills in two weeks. Am
really quite encouraged. I was glad to hear they are
getting along better at Franks. But Im sure I don't
know what Bertha will do if she cant get help. I know
Clarence is just as sweet and cunning as he can be. I

wish I could get hold of him. I have just heard a boat whistle. May be she brings me a letter from you. It is so late I dont suppose I will hear from the office tonight. Every one keeps early hours in Golconda.

It has been snowing all the afternoon but melting about as fast as it came  I hope it will turn into a rain, for we need it so much. The dust has been perfectly fearful. The river is so low that only small boats can run The mails are very irregular, and every one says if the river doesnt rise, it will surely freeze, and then we may as well say goodbye to the rest of the world.

I was really glad to hear Nan Louterman has gone to her Uncles to attend school. She is a good girl and deserves a better chance than she has had the greater part of the time at home. Nov. 21 Sunday. Have just returned from Sabbath School. I think I must have had 70 or 75 in my class this morning.

I did not think when I laid down this letter the other morning that I should let a whole week pass. But this last week I have been so busy I could not find a minutes time to write. We have been invited out three evenings this week. and Thanksgiving day we had company here.

I spent a very pleasant Thanksgiving, but think the dinner would have tasted a little better if I had eaten it at home. I should have given thanks for a holiday if nothing else. I have 95 named now. Average about 83 or 85. I think it is too much for any one person to do.

One of the girls in Mr. Newcombs room hears three classes. two in the forenoon and one in the afternoon. But Im not sure but it bothers me more than it helps me.

I received another letter from you night before last.

I will try not to let so long a time pass again without writing. It is not likely we will be invited out so many evenings in the week again for months. It is a very quiet place. Usually there is nothing in the world going on evenings.

I am glad you have taken that little boy. He will be company for you, and if he is such a boy as you say, Im sure you will love him.

I have not heard from Sarah yet I dont understand why she dont write, unless she is returning evil for evil. I am needing my things badly especially my hat. I have nothing but my summer hat. I am going to write to her again to day. Ill tell her to do as she thinks best about getting a plume.

Sometimes I have half a mind to send for a merino. They are so cheap and may be they will be fashionable next winter.

And so Albert wants to write me. Send him my address I want to show him I can do better than I did before and make him forget that unfortunate laugh of mine.

To be sure I dont get very much time to write but I enjoy getting letters so much.

I am going to write to Bertha to day. Good bye for now

Love to all.

Mary

I begin already to count the months before I will be at home.

Notes: Clarence is the first born of Bertha and Frank Bice. He was probably named after Bertha's brother, Clarence Owen, the Civil War letter writer. Clarence Bice only lived two years. He was born in 1868 and died in 1870.

*******************************

Golconda, December 5th 1869.

Dear Father & Mother,

I received a letter from Bertha containing a postscript from you, Ma, just a week ago tonight I had just written that day to both you and Bertha. I presume you have received both of the letters ere this. I have not received my home letters this last week but can excuse this for I can guess the reason. You have been over taking care of Bertha. I want to say right here Bertha's letter came through in three days. It was mailed at Springfield.

My compliments to the little stranger over at Bertha's. I haven't found any name too suit me yet.

What or who does it look like? I dont believe I will ever love it half as well as I do little <u>Clarence</u>. Is it as pretty as he was, and as good? Was Bertha a good girl? Oh dear, I just want to come up and see it, the baby, and not the girl. What does Clarence think of it?

One more month of school is gone. Only several more. Sometimes I think maybe we wont have to teach but nine months after all. They have such very warm weather down here it will be pretty hard to teach into the middle of July.

I haven't heard a word from Sarah yet. Am needing my hat very badly. It is now two weeks since I wrote the last time. I should think she might write to me anyway, if she did nothing more. We have been having the gloomiest weather, dont think we have had more than three pleasant days for three weeks. Almost every day it is so dark when school closes I can not see to read or write at my table. My school increased beautifully I have had two new scholars this last week.

We have monthly reports here the same as they do at Normal. Every time they come around to be filled out I tell you we have to work. Usually all the time we can get from Friday night till Monday morning it takes to get them done. I speak of it because this last week finished out another month and we were at work all day yesterday. Mine are not nearly done yet. Just think of making out reports for 88 or 90 pupils each one having four or five studies.

I feel so sorry for Grace, from what Bertha wrote me, I guess she does not find it like home back there. It seems as if her trouble would be hard enough to bear if she had all the sympathy and help friends could give her.

Are you and Mrs Shreve as neighborly as you were last summer? I declare, you both of you ought to be ashamed neglecting your families to run about as you do!

I suppose Aunt Mary has as great a passion for visiting as we

Has she been down since I came away. I dont know when I'm going to get time to write to her. Christmas I guess.

It is four o'clock and I ought to write two more letters tonight so goodbye for this time.

I shall look for a letter from you tonight. The river is up now and we get mail regularly every day.

Love to all, take good care of your selves.

Mary

Notes: Aunt Mary is Abigail Leach Owen's (Mary's mother's) sister. The baby being talked about in this letter is named May.

\*\*\*\*\*\*\*\*\*\*\*\*\*\*\*\*\*\*\*\*\*\*\*\*\*\*\*\*\*\*\*\*\*

Golconda. December. 19.1869.

My Dear Parents.

I am ever so busy today, if it is Sunday. Next Wednesday examinations commence and we are very busy getting topics ready.

I have to print all of mine, for the children can neither write nor read writing. They print though, very nicely! They have to print all of their spelling lessons.

I have so little time I shall have to write a short letter, but I know you will expect one so I try to write at least a few words every week.

I received your last letter Thursday I sent one to you the day before. I do not understand why you dont get my letters. I write every week almost always on Sunday. If not then either Monday or Tuesday.

Your letters come very regularly now.

I presume you have my last letter before this. I asked you to write to Sarah about my hat and dress. I have written to her twice and she has not answered either. I have nothing but my summer hat to wear and dont want to get anything else of course. Besides I couldnt get anything if I did here. Next week we have vacation and if I had my dress I could make it my self. After school commences there is no use of talking I dont get a minutes for sewing, not more than enough to do my mending. Almost every day it is dark when we get home

Notes:   The rest of this letter is missing. There are multiple letters in the same envelope addressed to Jason Owen Esq Elkhart Illinois and the postmark is Golconda Ill Mar 23.

\*\*\*\*\*\*\*\*\*\*\*\*\*\*\*\*\*\*\*\*\*\*\*\*\*\*\*\*\*\*\*\*\*

Golconda. Jan. 9. 1870

My Dear Parents.

Your letter has just reached me. You did not say anything about hearing from me. presume my letter has reached you before this time.

I was so sorry to hear that Mrs Shreve was so low. I can hardly think of anything else. I do hope she is better.

I am feeling so well now. Am as fleshy. I havent been as well for a year. School has commenced again. Every thing is going off nicely I have sent a class of 19 into Alice's room. and still have a room full left. I am going to teach a good school this term. I can see how to do a good many things better than last term. Pa, I wish you and Ma could come in my school. I know you would like it.

I dont teach one bit as I did when I taught before. I think now I have as nice a little school as you can find anywhere.

I have had to work awful hard and do yet for that matter. The time now is almost half gone. Do you want me to promise to come back here next year?

I had a letter from Sarah this last week. She told me about having written twice before. I think she must have made some mistake in directing her letter. I had written her again and sent the letter before hers came. I asked her to send me some samples again. I thought maybe I would hear from her again today or tomorrow.

I thought you had sent her money to get the things. I understood so from your letters. Newcomb said maybe the reason I did not get her letters that they had been opened. some one thinking the samples of dress goods was money.

We have got a little baby boy here. Mrs Charlie McCoys It was born last Tuesday. Is as pretty a little baby as I ever saw.

You did not say whether Bertha's baby was pretty or not. I am sorry it is so cross, for I think she would have her hands full, if the baby was as good as Clarence used to be

I am only going to write a short letter this time. I shall feel anxious until I hear from you again about Mrs Shreve.

Ma do favor yourself all you can. I know it is pretty hard to do when there is only one to do everything.

And now I must say goodnight with love to all.

Write soon.

Mary.

Notes: This was in the same envelope as the Dec. 19, 1869, partial letter.

*********************************

Golconda. Feb. 7. 1870

My Dear Parents.

Yesterday's mail brought me another letter from you. the second since I have written you. I have been so busy I have not had time to think of you, let alone writing. Tonight I am only going to say a few words so you will not worry about me. This is Monday night. We have no school this week. The Institute commences tomorrow afternoon I have to take a class and illustrate the word method of reading. Thursday night we have the exhibition. I dont think I could give you any idea of the work I and all of us have had to do this last week. I dont think I was in bed a single night before half past eleven. Tonight is the first night I have had to myself for two weeks and the only way I happened to get this was by working all of to day on exhibition. I think we are going to have a very good one.

I had a letter from Sarah a little over a week ago. my dress came a week ago today. I am very much pleased with it. It fits very nicely without altering at all. I haven't had time to touch it. I am so much obliged to her for doing what she has. I like the way it is made so much.

A letter came from Bertha the same time Sarah's came. I shall answer it as soon as I can.

Beside all the rest of the work this week we have our monthly reports to make out. I will try and write again next Sunday. and tell you about the exhibition I don't know what I'm writing and I think it is very doubtful if you do after reading this.

I'm awful tired. Love to all and a big lot for yourself.

Write every week<br>Mary.

******************************

Golconda Jan. 2. 1870.

My Dear Parents.

A little over a week has passed since I sent my last letter. and I know you expecting to hear from me all of the time. Our holiday is over, and tomorrow we commence another term. I am not sorry either. I feel rested and well again. This short rest has been very acceptable. I dont know that I was ever more thoroughly worn out than when school closed I must go back to the time my last letter was sent and tell you about examinations. Everything went off very nicely indeed. With the exception of unpleasant weather. everything passed off as pleasantly as I could wish. I shall not dread another examination. I did this for it was something new to me, in the capacity of teacher, and I didn't know exactly how much I could do, or rather, what I could do, or the children either. Examinations commenced Wednesday morning and closed Thursday afternoon.

Friday we helped the Sabbath school superintendent, Mr Sloan get the presents and Santa Claus ready. I did not think of receiving a present that evening. but did get two. A pair of very handsome vases from the Sabbath school and a shell box from one of my day school scholars. In the box I found a lot of nice candies and a pair of pearl sleeve buttons.

Christmas morning I had a good many presents. Mr. Newcomb gave me a book. Alice a silver thimble Mr. Howard McCoy a very nice knife Mrs. McCoy a little sephyr cup or dewdrop. I dont know what you would call it hardly, but it is just as pretty as can be. Mamie a box of paper cuffs Mr Charles McCoy a bottle of choice perfumery. Mrs. C. McCoy a book. Johnnie Gilbert, a school boy brought me a large basket of southern fruit Oranges, dates, figs and bananas. I thought of you and wished I could share them with you.

I had a pleasant Christmas but that did not make me forget you or that this the first Christmas I ever passed away from home

I was very sorry to hear Bertha is getting along poorly. I do hope she will let everything go and take care of herself.

I am real glad Sarah has written to me, although I have not received the letters. I had begun to feel a little hard toward her. not one word and she must know that if I ever needed my things I would want them before this time.

Last Tuesday I went to the milliners and bought a frame and some trimmings total cost $1.35 and made me a hat. Of course it isn't anything nice. I don't even like it but now down here it wont be but a little while till I will want something for summer and I dont think it is worth while to get another hat.

They tell me that very often in April they wear the thinnest summer clothing. As for the dress I need that, and shall have to have one. Ill tell her to send something that would do now and till late in the Spring too. I'm going to write to Sarah to day and have her send samples again I'll give her my address she must have made some mistake in directing her letters. Tell my little brother I think of him and want to see him and hope he will help Pa and Ma all he can till I come home.

Mary.

**********************************

As soon as we get school in running order again Ill write.

About money, never mind that I can get along well enough till April I guess.

Now take good care of yourselves and think that the time is almost half gone that I have to stay here. We have just made out our fourth monthly report.

I am going to try next term to teach a better school than ever before. If instead of 100 pupils I had 65 or 70, I'd like it.

And now good bye
With love to all
Mate

Notes: This letter was in the same envelope as the one above and addressed to Jason Owen, Esq. Elkhart, Illinois. The postmark is Golconda Ill. and stamped May. Also in the envelope was a receipt that goes as follows:

(18) UNITED STATES EXPRESS COMPANY.
Elkhart Jan 29 1870.
Received of Jason Owen 1 Jar said to contain Butter valued at --------- Dollars, and marked Mrs J H Owen Normal Ills
Which we undertake to forward to the nearest point of destination reached by this Company only, perils of navigation excepted. And it is hereby expressly agreed that the said UNITED STATES EXPRESS COMPANY are not to be held liable for any loss or damage, except as forwarders only; nor for any loss or damage of any box package or thing, for over $50 unless the just and true value thereof is herein stated; nor for any loss or damage by fire, the acts of God, or of the enemies of the Government the restraint of governments, mobs, riots, insurrections, or pirates, or from any of the dangers incident to a time of war; nor upon any property, or thing, unless properly packed and secured for transportation; nor upon fragile fabrics, unless so marked upon the package containing the same; nor upon any fabrics consisting of, or contained in glass.
FOR THE PROPRIETORS,          E. L. Cotton
Agent.
47 pounds

*******************************

Wednesday Evening Feb. 23 1870
My Dear Mother
I have just finished reading Pa's letter of Feb. 18. He tells me that you and Bertha are up to Normal

Of course you had a pleasant visit. Did you visit school while you were there. You must tell me all about your trip. How did you find Abbie's folks, and Sarah's? The last letter I had from Sarah she was not feeling well. I answered her letter nearly two weeks ago. have been expecting an answer for two or three days. Presume your visit has something to do with the delay. She said to write if I wanted the ruffles and as I concluded to have them I wrote immediately. It took away all the pleasure of Pa's letter to hear that Frank thought of going to Kansas. I suppose it will be a good thing for him financially but it does seem to me as if I never could be reconciled to it.

I am going to write them tonight. Does he think of taking Bertha and the children this Spring? Why if he did I would not see them again. I cant bear to think of it.

Ma, I have something to say to you and hardly know how to do it. If I could only see you I could make you understand how it is. But what I put down on paper stares at me so. It seems as if some one was saying it over after me You know I said in my last letter I had something to tell you. I couldn't do it then, and it does not seem much easier now only that the enclosed letter to Pa tells it for me. I know you will be very much surprised, and I am afraid you will think I am hasty, or do not know my own mind. I know, too, that he is an entire stranger to you I have not even mentioned his name in my letters, since that unlucky time in Bertha's letter, for which you both gave me such a proper talking to. What can I say now, if I tell you what others think of him here, you will say I am not an impartial judge. I can only say he is a great deal better than I am, and I dont know how it happened that he likes me but he thinks he does, and Ma, I love him with my whole heart; and I know he is worthy. Do not be angry or think I have done wrong. You do not know how happy it will make me if you and Pa will consent to our engagement, or at least not forbid it until you know him, and then I am not at all afraid.

I would like to have you know what Newcomb thinks of him, but you see it would not be very pleasant for us, if you were to make enquiries of him. In the paper I send you will find Mr. Sloan's name mentioned in the description of the proceedings of the Institute

I am feeling quite well now. We have lived through the Institute and Exhibition and have nothing now but our every day work.

I shall look for a letter from you as soon as next Sunday

With lots of love to all

Mary.

Ma, dont let even Frank and Bertha see this.

Notes: This was in an envelope addressed to Mrs. Jason Owen, Williamsville, Illinois. The postmark is Chatham Ill Feb 22.

I believe the Abby she is talking about is the wife of Mary's half-brother Warren Owen.

\*\*\*\*\*\*\*\*\*\*\*\*\*\*\*\*\*\*\*\*\*\*\*\*\*\*\*\*\*\*\*\*\*

Golconda March 20. 1870

My Dear Father & Mother.

Ere this you have received the letter I wrote to Bertha a week ago today. I thought then I should write certainly in a day or two. But I have been almost sick, and very busy. The weather is so changeable now that there are a great many sick from taking cold.

Dear Father and Mother, your full and free consent, and the confidence you place in me have made me very happy. And I hope that not only now, but always, I may show myself worthy your trust and love. When your letters came I came up to my own room and read them over and over again. I almost felt as if it were wrong for me to think of leaving you. That my first thoughts and care should be for you, who have done so much for me. But Ma, you are right. you are not losing me. for you are nearer and dearer to me than ever before. but gaining a son One who hopes in part, to fill the place of one who has gone before. Today it seems a long, long time before I can see you. but almost two thirds of the time is gone, and I suppose the remaining three months will pass as the ones before have done. It is only a little while now till examinations again. I do not dread them this time I know my school have done well this time. I wish you could come in my school. I have two little classes in drawing now. they do first rate.

The children here are the most affectionate children I ever saw. I dont know how many there are that are fully determined to go home with me.

I am obliged to write a short letter this time for Will has given me a letter for you, and it makes the letter so large to use any more paper. I want to send his letters in this way for every one here knows his writing, and at the P. O. they are a little more curious about other peoples business than necessary. so if he should direct a letter to you they would be sure to know it.

Write me right away.

With lots of love to all, and kisses for the little ones

Mary.

Notes: This was in an envelope addressed to Jason Owen, Esq. Elkhart, Illinois with a postmark of Golconda but a Feb date. She wrote this letter on one piece of paper and when she had filled the sheet she turned it sideways and began writing in that direction over what she had already written. She did this on many of her letters, saving paper. There was no other letter in the envelope.

\*\*\*\*\*\*\*\*\*\*\*\*\*\*\*\*\*\*\*\*\*\*\*\*\*\*\*\*\*\*\*\*\*\*\*

Golconda. April. 2. 1870

My Dear Mother,

I am very, very tired tonight, but know I shall feel rested after having a talk with the home folks. Today we have made out the schedules for six months. I had 107 names on my roll, so you can have some idea of the work to be done. We commenced early this morning and finished a few minutes ago. It is now 8. o clock

Frank's and Bertha's letters came last evening. You may be sure they were warmly welcomed. All the more so because I was not feeling well. I was not well enough to be in school yesterday afternoon and was rather "blue" Dont go to worrying about me for it is nothing serious, and I am much better to day. I am taking medicine all of the time.

Tell Frank and Bertha they dont know how glad I am that Frank has made up his mind to stay here for the present.

Will has given me a letter for you, after reading it I told him I wouldn't send it, for you would be sure to think I had been careless, and that isn't so, only in that instance, I have worn thick shoes all of the time, this Winter, and have takens care of myself in every way better than I ever did before in my life. But he declared if I didn't send it he would, so I concluded I had better send it, if it was to go, and tell you how things are.

I am glad Sarah and Lou came down and spent their vacation with you. I was surprised at first to see Lou's letter mailed at Elkhart. I have not heard from Sarah since she went home. Thought may be she would write this week. So that letter was not lost after all. I had made up my mind I should not hear from that again. I  shant send any more money in letters any way.

Peach trees are almost in blossom, in fact some are in blossom. They say it is much later this year than usual In about two weeks now Golconda will be another Eden. That reminds me of something. The other day, I came across an article in a Chicago paper, containing a short description of Golconda, and of a gentleman living here, whose son is an acquaintance of mine. I will look it up and send it.

Don't think because I use so many pieces that I'm out of paper. I thought at first that a half a sheet would be all I could send. But Ill put this in anyhow.

I shall try to answer Frank and Bertha's letters this next week. don't know whether I will succeed or not for we will be very busy until after examination. I have had a Major General in visiting my school twice this last week. Gen. Raus  He was pleased to be quite flattering in his remarks.

Golconda has been a busy little town for the last two weeks. Court has been in session and there are a great many strangers in town.

A new boat, "The Idlewild" enters in this trade this next week. Mr. Gilbert, one of the citizens here, has a large share in her. We, the teachers of the Golconda school, have an invitation, through him, to take the round trip on her, that is, down to Cairo, and up to Evanville and back.

Every one down here makes a great fuss over a new boat, when it first comes out.

I have not got the river fever very badly yet but still I like to see them.

But it is bedtime, and more too, for since I commenced this letter, Mrs McCoy came up and I talked with her a long time.

I wish I could be with you tonight, but never mind, this is the second day of April and if we dont have vacation we will close on the first day of July, so I must be patient only a little longer.

Remember me to all of my friends.

Love and kisses for you all , a large share of the kisses for the little ones. I will trust you to give them to them. Write soon

Mary.

Mon. morn.

As I have not sent this I thought I would tell you that I fell as good as new this morning.

Don't worry about me. write soon

Notes: This also was in the same envelope as the Dec. 19, 1869, partial letter.

\*\*\*\*\*\*\*\*\*\*\*\*\*\*\*\*\*\*\*\*\*\*\*\*\*\*\*\*\*\*\*\*

Golconda. April 14, 1870.

My Own Dear Father and Mother.

Your letter came yesterday morning. I had so looked and longed for a letter from home. I came up stairs that I might enjoy it all alone. As I opened the letter I happened to glance at your letter, Pa, first. It seemed to me that I was powerless to lift my eyes until I had read it all. I have felt ever since like one in a horrible dream. Oh, if I could only come home and help you bear it. You did not say a word about Frank and Bertha. Are they with you yet? It seems to me as if any other trouble in the world, I could have borne better. I feel, Oh so hard and bitter.

It is cruel, wicked, wrong that our good name, our all, should be taken from us. I thought I understood James's disposition thoroughly. I know how careless, thoughtless, easy, yes and selfish under all, he is. But that he would do such a thing as that, never, Pa, there must be some mistake.

I feel as if I could not stay here another day. Poor, poor Sarah. When I think of her, I feel ashamed of myself. What is my little trouble compared with hers. What does she intend to do? Will she stay there in Normal? Do people know about it there. What is Charlie doing? I hope and pray this trouble may make a man of him.

I gave Will the letter last night. I could not tell him, but wrote a note telling him, if after reading your letter, he so wished, to consider himself free from any engagement. I have not seen him since, but my own dear father and mother, if the worst comes, I am still sure of two hearts, whose love nothing can change. I can not write more tonight. I do not know that you can read what I have written, for I can not see my paper half of the time.

My love to Bertha and Frank. Tell them I have not had a minutes time to write them, but now hope I shall not be so busy and now goodnight. I may not send this tomorrow. If I do not I shall write a few more words. I shall see Will tomorrow night.

Since I wrote the first of this I have read your letter over carefully and tried to think how such a thing could happen. I can not thing that he did not intend to pay for them. You know how sanguine he is, he probably did not make money as fast as he expected. Do you know any of the particulars? When does his trial come off. Has he employed any counsel

Surely if they can prove that he intended to pay for them it will be all right. If you go his security cant he get out of jail. Write and tell me all you know about it. About the money. We have drawn seven months pay. After paying my board I will send all home that I do not want. I had rather do it than be troubled with it here of course.

Ma, I have not written to Sarah yet. I want to send to her for some things had I better. You wanted to know if I had to make up the time no. We made the Winter term longer, so this term will not be quite three months.

Don't worry about me, Ma, I am much better, but still under the Dr.'s care and a very good Dr. he is too. It is my old trouble that I had last Summer is the cause of all I think. But that was something entirely different from what we thought I wish you would write immediately I do so want to know all that you know about that. I look for another letter from you to day
With love and kisses

Mary.

Notes: This was also in the same envelope as the Dec. 19, 1869, partial letter. As stated earlier, it is believed that Sarah was Sarah Camel, and James was her husband. It is possible, however, that either James or Sarah was another Owen child, though there is no other evidence that they had any more children. We also do not know what James' misdeed was. This could be the same James mentioned in one of Warren's letters. He apparently suffered from sticky fingers, but there is no other evidence that they are the same person.

We do not know the identity of Will. He and Mary were apparently engaged. She does mention Will in a later letter, but not whether they were still engaged, and there was never a wedding announcement.

*******************************

Golconda. April 29. 1870.
Dear Father, Mother, Brother, and Sister,

Pa's letter came last
night. I don't know why, but just as soon as the letter
was put in my hand, I felt there was sad news for me.
It seemed to me, I had not strength enough to open
the letter.
I can not realize it yet. I shall not until I come home,
and miss the bright laughing face, the busy hands the
dainty kisses, the sweet baby ways. My dear brother
and sister, my heart aches for you. If I were only with
you, if I could only see you and help you bear this
great sorrow. I know how dark all seems now, and the
heart refuses to receive comfort. Let us not forget the
present, but let us look beyond. "Yet a little while",
and we shall see our dear little Clarence just as we
saw him here. In the meantime, we know a loving
Father watches over him.

Sunday Afternoon. Ma, your letter came this
morning, before Sunday school. I wanted to write this
morning but I had to learn my Sunday school lesson,
and as I stayed to Church after Sunday school was
over, this is the first leisure time. I suppose it was all
for the best that you did not send for me for it is more
than likely I would not have received the telegram in
time to get home to see him. But it seems as if it
would not have been quite as hard to give him up if I
could have seen him once more.

I shall feel very anxious about you until I hear
again. If you have not time to write me a long letter,
and I know you must be very busy, send just a few
words every day or two.

Ma, you don't say anything about yourself. I
know you must be almost worn out. I know very well
how little rest you allow yourself to take, if any one is

sick. If I <u>could</u> only come home. But I must be patient, wait and work on for two more months.

I am going to send my money home this week. I should have done it before, but have neglected it.

O! if something could be done for James, maybe if he were free again he could make all right.

Dear brother, and sister, write to me just as soon as you can.

I wish I could help you to see the light beyond this dark cloud, say something that would help to lighten a little this great burden of sorrow it has pleased God to put upon us, but my own heart is too sad, and the words of comfort I fain would speak, grate harshly on my ear, and die unspoken on my lips.

I do so want to come home. I want you to promise me if anything <u>should</u> happen, if any of you should be very sick, to send for me, and do not wait too long.

I can not think of it. I get hard rebellious, and bitter, when I think of any of my dear ones being taken away. I must say good bye now. Kiss little May. Never again in this world can I kiss our dear little Clarence. I know it is better for him, but we would have cared so tenderly for him here.

Write me often.

Your loving
Mary.

Notes: This letter was also in the same envelope as the Dec. 19, 1869, partial letter.

******************************

Golconda, May 7. 1870

My Dear Parents,

I did not get any letter from you Sunday, nor any last week I presume you were waiting to hear from me and did not get my last weeks letter in time to write, as Mr McCoy carried it around in his pocket sometime after I gave it to him to mail.

This pen scratches so I can hardly make a mark. I should have written Sunday but was feeling so badly I didn't do anything but lie around, and be lazy.

Will wanted to write with me this time but they are having court here and he is very busy.

What are you all doing up there? Are Sarah and James with you? and Bertha and Frank. Bertha owes me a letter. It seems as if the time never would pass I want so much to see you. I suppose though the first of July will make its appearance after a while. I am very busy now, and ought to be in bed now for it must be 11 o'clock. You will get only "How do you do" and "Goodbye" this time. I thought maybe you'd rather have <u>that</u> than nothing.

Mrs. Newcomb has gone to her home up north. Mr Newcomb says he is going home with me to get acquainted with you. I wish he would. I know you would like him Dont know whether he is joking or not.

We have strawberries, peas, beets etc. in plenty, and have had them over three weeks. I suppose strawberries will be all gone again when I get home.

I am so tired I cant write any more tonight. may be I'll write in the morning. Love to all. Will always wants to be remembered to you.

He has just had some pictures taken. I think they are very good Ill send one. What I did send don't look at all like him.

Goodnight and love to all
Mary

Are they going to have a celebration in Elkhart the fourth? I want you to answer this right away. Send me four or five of those tin types.

*********************************

Golconda Feby 10th 1871

My dear Sister Mate

I have been thinking of writing you a letter for a week past. Tho most every night (the time I do <u>most</u> of my "loveletter" writing) my time is employed writing to Lucy. You owe me 2 or 3 letters now. tho a letter from Lu 2 weeks ago explained this. I was very sorry to hear you had been sick. tho I almost knew something was the matter as I had no letter from you. you are too good a sister not to write to me when you feel able. in fact you dare not wait so long when you can write, for you know you would get a good scolding. I hope Lu is with you before now. and <u>I</u> <u>hope</u> <u>too</u> she will be with <u>me</u> before a <u>great</u> while. and you too. dont you feel better since she arrived at your house? and are you not well enough to come home with her? you know how <u>fat</u> you got the first time you came here after you had been here a while? & before you had to work so hard? if you will come down with Lu you will be <u>well</u> in short time. I do hope you can come. I want to see you , so do many more of your friends. I wrote to Lu to come via Bloomington, for if she comes that way, she will have no change to make after leaving B. & no lay over at Centralia going south. and if go via St Louis have to remain there about 2 or 3 hours. and any way as you are coming home with her by your going via B. you can tell how you can stand the trip by the time you get to B. I hope you will get ready soon. I want to see Lu muchly tho do not wish to drive her away from your house it seems to me she has been gone a good long time <u>and</u> <u>she</u> <u>has</u> <u>too</u>!

the school is progressing nicely. all well at Charleys
Fathers. Newcombs.
My kindest regards to your Father  mother Mrs & Mr
Bice. Kiss Lucy for me and accept just one from
Your Bro
Thos
Hows the Ranch?


Notes:   This was in the same envelope as the one titled
Golconda May 9th 1871.
Mate is the nickname for Mary Owen. Thomas is not really her
brother, but rather an affectionate term for a close friend. Thomas and his
wife Lucy are the folks with whom Mary boarded when she lived in
Golconda.

*******************************

Golconda Feby 16th 1871
My dear friends Mr and Mrs Owen
As I attempt to write to you (this my first letter)
it seem my heart will burst, at the sad news from my
wife, but a moment ago. Oh dear, but I wish I could
find words to express to you (two heart broken
parents) my feelings of the death of our dear, good
sister and friend Mate. I never had such feelings but
once before. the death of my sister. It does seem very
hard to know she has gone, and I cannot realize it. I
had no idea she was at al dangerous, and but
yesterday, I wrote her a long letter (sent to my wife'
address) urging Mate to come home with Lucy. how
awful it must be to you all. I know something of your
feelings, by my owen.
Why, I should feel so? May seem strange, to
you. No one not even our dear friend Mate knew how
much Lucy & I thought of her. any thing I could have

done as a true friend, would have been, to have made her happy and my wife's feelings are the same. I regret <u>very</u> much that I did not know how near death she was. I only wish I could have seen her once more. We have calculated very much (ever since I was with you) to have Mate come to our home. I wanted her to come with me while there. and now, regret very much she did not, for I truly believed she would be well by coming here. the day before Mates death Lucy writes me, "Mate has not read your letter yet, but says it will make her better when she gets it" and speaks to (Mrs Owen) how kind you were to her. I only wish Mate had recd my letter and her words proven true. My friends, every one of you, have my heart felt sympathy. My wifes letter (a few moments after receiving it). I read to our friend Mrs Newcomb. and my Bro & Wife. their feelings, I can assure you, expressed. their love for Mate. Many good friends of Mates in Golconda will be shocked. One request I wish to make of you well you please. burn all the letters we wrote to Mate? Some day I hope to meet you again & will explain why. one reason <u>now</u> is, I expressed my utter contempt for some people to her. and would prefer to have them burned. My kindest regards to Mr and Mrs Bice & the little girl a kiss, and for you accept the kindest wishes

From your<br>
True Friend<br>
Thomas W Mc

Notes: This was also in the same envelope as the May 9<sup>th</sup> 1871, Golconda letter.

 This, again, was a shock to our family as we read the letter. Mary seems to have died from a long illness, though we have no idea the nature of that illness. The illness could account for the fact that there are no letters after May 7, 1870.

Thomas and Lucy McCoy are the couple that Mary roomed with while teaching in Golconda. Mr. and Mrs. Bice are Bertha and Frank and the little girl is their daughter May.

********************************

Normal, Ill., Feb. 21, 1871
Mr. Jason Owen and Family;
Elkhart,
Illinois.,
Dear Friends;
I am instructed by the Philadelphian Society of the Normal University, of which the late Miss Mary E. Owen was a member, to send to you the enclosed resolution adopted by that Society.
Yours truly,
Louise Ray,

Chairman Com.

Normal, Feb. 21. 1871.
Whereas an All-wise Providence has seen fit to remove from earth our friend and sister Philadelphian, Miss Mary E. Owen, therefore
Resolved that we recognize the loss sustained not only by the family of the deceased, but by this society.
Resolved that the Philadelphian shall be draped in mourning for 30 days in token of our respect for her memory.
Resolved that the society express its sympathy for the bereaved friends by sending them a copy of these resolutions.

Resolved that these resolutions be placed on the records of the society, and be published in the Bloomington Pantagraph and the Chicago Schoolmaster.

                                    Louise Ray,
                    Committee.   Lottie C.
Blake,
                                    J. P. Yoder.


Notes: There is an Illinois State University, in Normal, Illinois today. At one time, the Normal School, or Normal University was a part of the Illinois State University, or the Illinois State Normal University. There is no mention of a Philadelphia Society at the University today. Descriptions of Normal Schools, and of the Philadelphia Society, can be found on the Internet.

********************************

J.W. McCoy,
        Tom W. McCoy.
        OFFICE OF

**J.W. McCOY & SON,**

DEALERS IN

**PORK, GRAIN AND PROVISIONS.**

Also Manufacturers and jobbers of

No. 1 Shaved Cypress Shingles.
ORDERS SOLICITED
        AND
Promptly Filled.

Golconda, Ills., Feby 23 1871

Mr and Mrs Owen

Dear Friends

To day I mail you our paper . . . doubtless you would have recd one any way, as I subscribed for it, for one year, for our dear departed Mate . . . I cannot realize that Mate is gone. . I regret very much I was not there, a letter from Mrs McCoy, tells me, she has one of Mates pictures and having it enlarged. . I am truly glad to know this. . the morning after I recd the sad news, and while, the school was at devotional exercises in Mr Newcombs room, the present teacher (of Mates room) announced the death of Mate, every little one left the room crying & near all in the room did the same. . every one in the school of her acquaintance loved her. . although she is gone, it is a pleasure to know how every one loved her. . this is consolation. I go to Cairo to day to meet Mrs McCoy . my kindest regards to Mr & Mrs Bice and love to the little girl. . accept my best wishes always.

Your friend

Tom McCoy

Notes: This was also in the same envelope as the Dec. 19, 1869, partial letter.

\*\*\*\*\*\*\*\*\*\*\*\*\*\*\*\*\*\*\*\*\*\*\*\*\*\*\*\*\*\*\*\*

Golconda May 9th 1871

Mr and Mrs Owen

Dear Friends

It has been some time since I wrote to you, tho I hope my silence will never cause you to think you are Forgotten. We think of you very often, and of our dear good departed friend Mate every day. We have a splendid picture of her framed and hanging in our sitting room. I wish it were so <u>she</u> could be there, tho I do not know as it is right to wish her here, but it seems at times she ought to be with us. We cannot realize yet, that she is gone. and it does seem strange to me yet, that such persons are taken & so many that are of so little use in the world are left, but so it is.

I should have written to you long ago, (for I have thought about it often) but I am so busy all the time. it is only occasionally that I get time to steady down & write to my friends. tho I may not write often, I want you to know, that you are <u>often</u> thought of, tho you may be ever so lonely since Mate died, you are <u>not</u> so, in many good friends.

I believe my wife wrote to Mrs Bice few days ago. she has not been very well this spring, and has been quite busy too this spring, I presume Mr Bice is with you yet. say to him that any time he should be any where near here, <u>not</u> to fail to call & see us. would like to see any of you here at any time. if Mr B ever comes to Cairo it is only a short trip from there to G. and on good boats. one of our packets leaving there every evening (excepting Monday) arriving here next morning. if I should chance to have occasion to pass by E., I shall surely stop over a short time. I would like very much to see all of you. and hope to some day.

do you get our Co paper regular? I subscribed for it for Mate and told our editor to direct to you. of course it is of little interest to you. tho occasionally you may see something in it worth reading. our school is progressing well, and I hope to keep Mr N. another year, tho he may not remain.

To day we are having a very hard rain, and is a very gloomy day. the rain (partly) was needed. our crop of wheat is suffering very much from rust & we

hear of complaints from many other parts of the
country.
My kindest regards to Mr & Mrs. Bice & a kiss
for May, and accept my best wishes for yourselves
from your True friend.
Thos W. McCoy
My wife wishes to be remembered kindly to you all


Notes: There are five letters in the same envelope addressed to
Mrs. Frank Bice Elkhart City Ill The postmark is Golconda Ill dated
May. There is also a picture enclosed of a man taken at Philip Wright's
Photograph Gallery, 512 N. Second Street, below Buttonwood,
Philadelphia. None of the letters identifies who he is. He looks to be in
his 20s-30s and appears to have blond hair. He also has a dimple in his
chin.

*********************************

Golconda Sep 16th 1871
Dear friends one & all.
Perhaps you think we have
forgotten you, by our long silence, but it is not so. & I
feel ashamed that your kind letter has been so long
unanswered, but I do not feel as if I am entirely
without excuse, as my health has been such I could
not write. & Thos has been nurse which partly
excuses him.
On the 25th of June, a blue eyed little daughter,
claimed our attention & love – which is freely given --
& the Mother & baby have claimed most of the
attention since then, though now I am beginning to be
myself again. I think I should have got along nicely,
had it not been for my breast rising & breaking, which
of course caused me a good deal of suffering. Also my
teeth have troubled me a great deal. I am going up the

river this week to have them all out. & have some that will not ache, so much for excuses.

We have a dear little baby, we call her Hattie, for an old school mate of mine. had it not been for Mamie's name, we should have called her <u>Mary Owen</u>, for the dear friend & sister. I can hardly realize that it is nearly seven months since Mary left us, though no doubt the time has seemed long & lonely to you. I dream of Mary quite often sometimes as sick & others, as in perfect health. Did you get the pictures in India ink? & do you like them? I would like one of that kind though I think very much of the one we have.

You spoke of our losing a sister. The Mrs McCoy whose death you noticed in the paper was of another family. no relative of ours. An Uncle of Mr. McCoy's died a few weeks since. His father & mother are in poor health. There is more sickness here, than has been known for several years. chills, bilious fevers, etc. It is <u>very</u>, <u>very</u> dry. it seems as if we must have rain soon. There has been a great deal of fruit. I have put up over 140 qts. of different kinds. Peaches were not as nice a usual, though we have had a good many nice ones. Won't some of you be coming to the State fair? If you do I wish you would make us a visit. DuQuoin is only four hours ride from Cairo. & a boat leaves there every day but Monday, passing here. Mr Newcomb has our school again this year. we have the same teachers excepting in the Primary. Mr. N. talks of opening kind of a Normal school here next year. How are your friends at McLean? My regards to them. How is little May? I suppose you are all together yet. <u>Baby calls</u>. & such calls have to be answered, so I will have to close, hoping you will not wait as long as I have, before writing. Thos is not well but perhaps he will write some. Mamie is very well, & starts to school tomorrow.

With much love to each of you.
I am truly your friend
L. A. McCoy.
My sister & family are well. She has two very fine
boys.

Notes: This letter was also in the same envelope as the
Golconda May 9, 1871, letter.

\*\*\*\*\*\*\*\*\*\*\*\*\*\*\*\*\*\*\*\*\*\*\*\*\*\*\*\*\*\*\*\*\*

Golconda Nov. 5th 1871
Dear friend Mrs. Bice.
A few days since I was made glad by receiving a
letter from you. also the pillow came. & as "delays" in
writing are "particularly dangerous", I will try & write
some while baby is asleep. but as her naps are very
short & uncertain usually, you may get only a short
letter. To say that I thank you for the sofa pillow
would be but a weak expression. I think it is beautiful.
& besides I value it so highly, for the givers sake, as I
feel it a present from my dear friend, who is gone. It
seemed almost as a gift from the dead. I thank you for
your share in the gift, it came safely.
No, it does not seem as if so much time had
passed, since we bid Mary a long farewell. nor can I
yet realize that we shall never see her again. there is
not a day that I am not reminded of her. her picture
hangs in our family room. I would like to see the one
you have. I hope I may sometime.
I do wish some of you or all could visit us. won't
you sometime? The great fires are the almost constant
theme for discussion now. how terrible they are. &
what an amount of suffering there will be all of this
winter. It seems almost a sin for us to make plans for
pleasure or profit, while there are so many suffering
for even comforts of life. We know very little of

suffering. We had a good many friends in Chicago. all have suffered more or less by the fire.

My baby is growing nicely & is as sweet & cunning as she can be, with the bluest eyes & fairest skin I nearly ever saw. A great pet with us of course, as well as a great care. I find my hands pretty full. I have very poor help. & so have a good deal of housework to do. We have had very dry weather, the river was never known to be so low. This is a dull place where so few boats run. & very small ones at that. There had been a great deal of sickness this fall, owing to the hot dry summer I suppose. Mamie has had a little sick spell, but not much. she attends school & is learning very fast. Mr. Newcomb is still here but will not remain another year. I presume Alice is well, but such a <u>stay</u> at <u>home</u> body. I hardly ever see her. their little boy is very smart. I am sorry May has been sick so much, but hope she will be well now. I would like to see the little rogue.

My sister & her children are in the country now. they were well. Harry is such a nice boy & understands so much. Hattie is crying & I shall have to close. Thos is not here, but would wish to be remembered to all.

I shall be <u>anxious</u> to <u>hear</u> <u>from</u> <u>you</u>. My kindest regards to your Mother, father, & husband. Write soon if you can

With love    your true friend
L. A. McCoy.

Notes: This was also in the same envelope as the Golconda May 9th 1871, letter.

It is clear that Thomas and Lucy McCoy were very close to Mary, as they kept in touch with her family nearly a year after her death, and mentioned her in every letter.

# Chapter 5 — 1878–1906

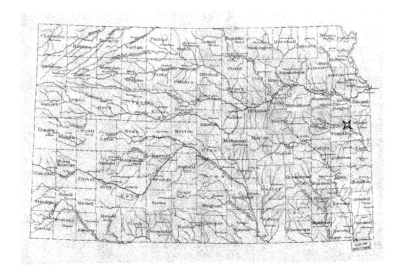

*Base map of Kansas*, 1893

Highlighted City: Wellsville

**Figure 10 — Kansas**

This chapter concludes the letters of the Owen family. They consist of letters to Bertha or Jason and Abigail, from family and friends, on a variety of topics; there is no general theme. They do bring the events of the Owen family up through the Bice family, and include the Dean family, which links to Jessie Dean Thackrey.

********************************

Eaton Oct 15, 1878

My Dear Brother a Sister
feeling lonely this Evening I thought I would take my Pen and converse with you for A few minutes and I hardly know what to write about as for myself I can say I am well and looking over the years that are past I can say the Lord in love has smitten and Chastized his erring one and while he wounds deeply how ready to heal the same kind hand that smites is ready to bind up the broken hearted, how I long for and wish I could see you that I might tell you all your Brother said (I see I began on the wrong leaf) and suffered in his last sickness it seems almost like A Dream to think he is gone and I have no more that I could do for him and yet during his sickness it was such A reality that I feel that I never could endure but I know he is at rest and happy with those that preceded him for in his troubled sleep he seemed to talk with Eliza and while my Brother Cyrenus his Wife was watching with him A few nights before he died he said Eliza I am coming home comforting to think he saw her as I believe he did he was so different in his last sickness it was A pleasure to do for him and Oh how much I saw every day something he has done to make things comfortable for us that remain to enjoy he had Faults like all of us but they are Buried and his good deeds appear greater to us now that he is gone from us

I thought when I received your last letter I should answer immediately for sometime after I wrote you Howard brought the last letter Chad carried it home and Linda did not say any thing to Howard about it as they had one soon after and she has had poor help in the House and no time only Sunday to write and then some of the Children came home and after they had gone she would be too tired to write  H and L was here last Sunday they came to hear Mr Gillis our Old Minister Preach you will remember him they was here to Dinner said she intended to write after she went home perhaps you have got the letter before this the weather is warm for the season you inquire after Charles Family they live Conn and now are doing well for A time he did not get much work but his Wife had plenty and good pay and he has had steady work the past year and they have only one Child She is 12 and is A good Scholar they have A good School and I hope they will be able to keep her in School there till she is fitted to teach as that is her ambition now Charles is in A Market and his Wife Embroiders Corsetts I am so glad the poor can find employment the times are some better then for the two years past remember me to all the Friends and let me hear from you often I hope Miles and Willie don't Flatter themselves they are to have anything from this unkle A for they will be disappointed if they do

Notes:   This was probably written by Mary Leach, wife of Augustin K. Leach. Augustin was the brother of Abigail Leach, who married Jason Owen. Augustin died in 1878. (Henry) Howard was another brother of Abigail's. Chad was one of Howard's sons. Linda (Rosalinda) was Howard's wife. Miles and Willie were sons of Adoniram, another brother of Abigail's.

\*\*\*\*\*\*\*\*\*\*\*\*\*\*\*\*\*\*\*\*\*\*\*\*\*\*\*\*\*\*\*\*

Elkhart Ind. Dec. 7th 1879.

My Dear Auntie & Uncle;

        The first Church bells are ringing and as I have a little time before going to Church, I am going to improve it by conversing with you through this silent medium. No doubt you have thought it strange you have not heard from me & wondered at the long silence. & I do not blame you at all and I am thoroughly ashamed of myself for not answering your dear good long letter rec'd so long ago. By Mother. She requested me to write and answer it for her which I promised to would do, and intended to have done so right away but days, weeks, and months have come and gone, and with its many household duties, its pleasures, of various kinds: and so forth and still your letter with many others has been self neglected. But I have thought of you dear Uncle & Auntie, and said so many times I must write, yet I trust you will forgive me & I will not dwell upon excuses & apologies, because I want to tell you of ourselves and how we are all prospering since last you heard from us, first I will say we were ever so glad to hear from you. But very sorry to hear you had had so much sickness in your family, but hope and trust you are all well again now. Yes we live in Elkhard, tho Father and Mother are still on a farm about three miles from here and still in the milk business. The farm where he is is sold now, & they expect to move on another farm near town, between now and January. It makes it very pleasant for me they being so near, for I see them nearly every day, that is Father, & Mother quite often, & I can go out home Just when I please. I am very pleasantly situated in town and have a good kind husband who does all he can for my comfort & happiness. I have no reason to be anything but happy, as I am blest with many good friends, a pleasant home and pleasant surroundings, and all which I appreciate very very much. I wish you could visit us in our cosy home, & hope you can some day.

Monday Evening. As I finished the above, I was obliged to lay it aside and go to Church, and we listened to a very interesting sermon from our Pastor, who always gives us good thoughts & ideas. We live about two blocks and a half from the Church so we go very regular, whether stormy or pleasant. We are not quite three blocks from Main Street, so you see we are nicely situated. My husbands Parents live but a short distance from us, also his brother who is married lives here, and we take a great deal of comfort going to see our parents and brothers and sisters. Brother Orrin is still in Chicago. He spent Thanksgiving with us. I invited thirteen here to dinner, those only of our nearest relatives. We had a very pleasant time, and in the evening, we had a surprise party which was gotten up by some of our people, they brought very nice refreshments which of course added greatly to the evenings entertainment, and all passed off very nicely, that evening was our anniversary & that was the way we celebrated its.

Cousin Clara Squiers came down from Chicago with my brother the evening before which I enjoyed very much.

Cousin Nellie Owen has not been down for some time but I expect her after the Holidays. I presume you have not heard of the death of Aunt Mary Jane, and no doubt this news will surprise you very much. She had been poorly for a long time, and the last four weeks of her life she had a great many hemorages & was confined to her bed. She failed very fast, and tho we did not think she could live so long as she did, yet we were startled when the news came. She died in the

Spring, I was there just four weeks before she died, when she was taken with her last sickness, we did not go to the funeral our people could not very well leave and I felt that I could not go again so soon, & thought perhaps it would be just as well for Nellie if I should go up some other time. My husband and I were up there in the fall, and the home seemed a very lonely one. You probably did not know that Aunt Jane married Mr. Howe, the husband of her sister (who died a few years ago). They had not been married two years I think when Aunt Jane died, but she had a pleasant good home and all the comforts one could wish for. Nellie still lives there and keeps house for Mr. Howe. She feels the loss of her Mother very deeply, & of course she would they had been together so many years. That to part them is sad indeed.

I rec'd a long letter from cousin Mary Armstrong Sat. saying her father had been quite sick with congestion of the lungs. But was better, but not well, Aunt Lucy is in poor health, has very severe sick spells occasionally.

Grandma has been with them considerable lately, but was in Hamilton when Mary wrote. she keeps quite well, tho fails very fast now Mary writes. I spent nearly three months East, a year ago last summer, & I had some very pleasant visits in my old home & with the many friends there. I wanted Grandma to come home with me and she rather wanted too, but some thought she better not, I am in hopes to see her out here this Winter, but don't know whether she will favor us with her company or not. George Allen & wife from Geneva Wis. Are now there, and he said if she would come with him he would be very glad to bring her. But I do hope she will come for we all want to see her so much.

Uncle Joseph and Aunt Helen still live in Hamilton. Uncle is in very poor health all of the time. Aunt Helen keeps usually well. their boys are both West, so they are quite alone and very lonely. The oldest one is in Chicago and doing very nicely, the other one has been here for some time till a few weeks ago he went to Goshen a few miles from here, and I don't know how he is doing now.

I have written you quite a lengthy epistle and for fear I will tire you I will close for the present. We would all love to see you dearly & hope we may some day. Perhaps it will be our good luck to visit you in your home & hope you all will come & see us.

I will enclose a great amount of love for Father Mother & Mother Owin, for you all, and also from my husband and myself, Write us soon if you are able to, & I will promise not to be so dilatory again. but please forgive me this time, for I love you all.

Your off. Niece Jennie E Smith.

Notes: This was in an envelope addressed to Mrs. A. H. Owen Elkhart, Illinois. The postmark is Elkhart, Ind. Dec 9th and on the back is a stamped note that says Received Dec. 10 Elkhart City Ill. Also included in the letter was the author's card which says Mrs. E. B. Smith.

\*\*\*\*\*\*\*\*\*\*\*\*\*\*\*\*\*\*\*\*\*\*\*\*\*\*\*\*\*\*\*\*

Sherburne Nov 27 1881

Dear Uncle & Aunt.
My very very Dear Friends.
Your very Kind & very good letter was duely received.
Although unexpected, it was none the less welcome, & meet with a most greatful & hearty reception.

We were indeed glad to hear from you, & know that you still live. How much we would like to see you. I said to our folk, after reading your letter, what I then felt & still feel, that I would give more to see you, than any other humans living.

I have long wanted to visit you, & see that section of country but it is very difficult for me to leave home; but should I ever again come west to make a visit among your friends, while <u>you</u> <u>live</u>, you may rest assured my first & objective point will be <u>your</u> house. But that I fear may never be for me too as well as yourselves are growing old. I am happy to be able & say however that we are all at present in the enjoyment of comfortable health & strength. You speak of hearing of Gennies severe sickness from Mrs Foot; She was indeed very sick & poorly for quite a long time, but she has I think fully recovered, & is now fleshy & stouter & stronger than ever before. There is so few of the old friends left in this part of the country that there is but little we can say about them. We occasionly meet some of the Lebanon folks Seamores & Wagoners folks were down & made us a visit not long since. Birdsel & his wife were down & staid all night with us in the fall, so we keep pretty well posted in regard to matters & things in Lebanon. And by the by Birdsel has got a right smart home for a wife I have been to, or rather through the hollow on the <u>railrode</u>, once or twice in as many years

Things in Lebanon as well as in this places have changed wonderfully since we were there.

Angie is in Philadelphia attending school. Ida is at home, & we are in hopes to keep her with us for a long time yet, some stories to the contrary not withstanding.

You speak of seeing or hearing from Mrs Foot, where are they now, we have not heard from them in a long

time. You say you have made a claim for a pention &
want to prove your marriage. I can most certainly
sware to that, for I shall never forget it nor the day; & I
hope you will succeed in securing the pention. Tell
your man to send on his papers, & please let us know
of your success in the matter.

All join in sending much love & hopeing to hear from
you again soon I will close by subscribing my self as
ever its eternally yours

Ira C Owen

Notes: This was in an envelope addressed to Mr. Jason Owen.
Elkhart Ill. with a postmark of Ranndallsville N.Y. but the date is Mar
20 and on the back of the envelope is a postmark Elkharton, Ill Mar 22
1880. Ira C. Owen was a doctor, born around 1823, with a wife named
Janette, daughters Ida F. and Angie N., and a son named Birdsall.
Birdsall Owen was living in Lebanon at this time with a wife named
Ophelia, daughters named Alice and Alleen and son Clarence. Birdsall's
name was recorded differently over the years in the census. In 1850 he is
listed as Burdell J, and in other records he is listed as Burrit. Ira was the
son of Jason's brother Josiah, and Josiah's wife Sally.

*********************************

Eaton Aug 27th 1882

Dear Cousin
I guess you will think that I dislike to
write letters because I do not answer any more
promptly I do not like like very well to write but I like
to receive letters as well as any one.

We have had very bad weather for the most of crops
this season Wet and cold untill about the 10 of July,
and since what it has been very dry, but with only a
few warm days had a fine rain last night and it has
rained a little today; we expect to commence picking
Hops in about one week we will not have a very large

crop but think that we will get a large price for what
we do have they are worth [there is a smudge so can't get the
first number] -.30 c per pound raw. I wish that you could
be here through Hop picking there is always lots of
fun in the Hop yards during the picking we expect to
be two weeks picking ours this year every body here
that can possibly get away goes Hop picking of course
they go for thier health but want to earn all that they
can pickers will make good wages this year the hops
are going to be good picking and when hops sell for a
good price we have to pay more a box for picking

Oats & Grass are a good here this year Corn will be
light Early Potatoes are small but think this rain will
help the later varieties Henry Baldwin Wife & Girl
made us a visit the week before last they thought that
they would get here for a couple of days last week but
they did not come Henry & I went fishing one morning
while they were here we did not have very good luck I
reckon it was not a good morning there was others
fishing but did not any of us catch many come down
here and you and I will see if we cant hook some fish I
dont see why you cant come here this Fall I will
garentee you a good time if you will come there is no
use of us working all of our days trying to get rich I for
one dont expect to ever be rich and not knowing how
long I shall live in this world I am going to try and
enjoy what money I earn

Get Scott & Hulda to come with you and all come
here this Fall will you you had better come and board
with me for 2 or 3 months for I am coming out there
again and I shall come with an appetite and if you
dont come here you will be behind      We went to
Barnums Show last Thursday it was a good thing and
a fearful crowd at 1 Oclock P.M. all of the Hotels
Eating houses &c were out of every thing that they
had to eat (could not even get a square meal) I

understood they sold 20000 show Tickets if the Show
comes near you it will pay you well to go if you never
saw it Write soon and come here as soon as you can I
would like ever so much to have you come and will
make it a pleasant visit for you if you will only come
you must excuse my writing I have had the
Rhumatism in my arm and shoulder for the last two
weeks so if you find a crooked mark where there
should be a strait one please dont mind it   Good Bye
for this time

Yours &c<br>H. B. Leach

\*\*\*\*\*\*\*\*\*\*\*\*\*\*\*\*\*\*\*\*\*\*\*\*\*\*\*\*\*\*\*\*

Eaton
Please direct to Eaton
Monday Evn'y
Charles Leach & his Wife were drowned Saturday
Afternoon about Sun down they drove into a pond to
wet thier Buggy Wheels drove in to far and tipped over
in the water thier little was with them but she floated
on the water untill a man got there and brought her
out Charles couldn't swim as he could have got out
without much dificulty he was one of Zenas Leaches
Boys we have been to this afternoon to thier Funeral
they were living about 9 miles from here at Madison
Adieu

Dot

Notes:  H.B. is Henry Burdette Leach, son of Henry Howard
Leach, and nephew of Abigail Leach Owen. Hulda could be the daughter
of Abigail's cousin, William H. Leach. William was the son of Ephram
Leach, Backus's brother. Charles Leach was the son of Zenas Leach,
another cousin of Abigail and the son of Ephram Leach.

\*\*\*\*\*\*\*\*\*\*\*\*\*\*\*\*\*\*\*\*\*\*\*\*\*\*\*\*\*\*\*\*

West Eaton Aug 31st 1892

My dear Aunt

I have sad news to write you this time
my Father was found dead in his bed last saturday
morning he went to Solsville with a grist of wheat to be
ground for flour for hoppicking and was as well as
usual and was laughing and talking till 9 oclock in the
evening He did not get up as he was in the habit of
doing while Carl was milking. He went in his bedroom
and spoke to him he did not answer so he knew he
was dead the Dr and coroner said it was Paralysis his
left side paralyzed they said he went to sleep and
never woke up he laid on his right side with his left
hand across him and his right hand up to his face the
bedclothes were just as he got in bed he looked just as
natural as could be

It was a great shock to all they were getting ready to
begin picking hops to day but rained so hard this
morning they did not go for the pickers but they have
just started to go for them

I am going to help Carls folks in hoppicking Clara is so
much better she can do the work with what her
husband can help her We will be so busy I can not
write any more Tress and her husband came out to
the funeral she is very poorly said she started right
away sat night after they got the telegram and staid in
Oneida over night then came here on sunday so she
did not wait to think she was not well enough to
endure the journey but she stood it very well

I must close

with love to all

Lib Leach

Notes: Libbie Leach was the wife of Horatio Leach, the son of Henry Howard Leach and nephew of Abigail Leach Owen.

\*\*\*\*\*\*\*\*\*\*\*\*\*\*\*\*\*\*\*\*\*\*\*\*\*\*\*\*\*\*\*\*\*

Wellsville, Kans.
June 3, 1893.

My Dear Mother:

I received your letter with one from Cora yesterday and to say that I was glad to get them does not nearly express it. I expected the letter on Tues. and was much disappointed when we came from Decoration services to find no mail at all for me. But I knew I would hear this week some time so it is all right. It must keep you all very busy to keep things going, any way since Cora has gone to B. From the way she wrote I thought she and Aunt S. were getting along very nicely. She wrote me all the news about every one there. Said Aunt S. had one little turkey which she would save for a roast for me, when I got home. By the way, did C. get the hdkf. I sent her some time after her birthday? I supposed she did but as none of you had spoken of it I thought it might have been lost.

So school closes next week does it? If you are not having better weather than we are I think it will be rather "damp" for a picnic. Will they make an "all day" affair of it or have it in the afternoon.

I suppose May and Eva both are expecting to attend the institute and board with Mrs. Orton. Tell E. to let the work go and give her studies a good review. I do not think she will have any trouble in getting a certificate, and I hope she will know something definite about the school soon.

Has Frank heard whether he passed or not yet? Don't forget to tell me if he has.

Mrs. J. is getting ready to go to take off some more chickens this A.M. She has about 562. Lost several since it has been so rainy and cool. She has several hens setting yet and every few days sets more. This has been a very rainy week but this morning the sun keeps breaking through so I think maybe it will clear off now. Sun. it was quite nice but rained that night and the next day; Tuesday morning it looked very much like rain but finally cleared off and proved to be as nice a day as one would want for Decoration Day. It rained again Tues. night and has every day since. Last night it poured down nearly all night. I do hope now, that we may have some nice weather for I know I would get better so much faster then. Mr & Mrs J. thought yesterday that I would be much better off if I slept upstairs, so they moved down into my room and gave me theirs up stairs and it did seem so different up there last night. I coughed less this morning when I got up than I have for a long while. Do not know whether the room had any thing to do with it or not but Mrs J. thinks it had for she said she never got rid of her cough until she went to sleeping upstairs.

The room I had did seem as damp and musty as could be for all I kept it aired all I possibly could.

I have never enjoyed a Decoration day as I did last Tues. They had no especial services at W. but the Soldiers graves at both cemeteries were decorated before the G.A.R's and S. of V's with their friends, took the train for Gardner (two stations above here) where they had been invited to observe the day. Mr & Mrs J. and I went besides 97 others. When we got there they had conveyances to take all the ladies to the cemetery, a mile distant and Mrs J. and I had the honor of riding in the carriage that headed the procession. When we returned it was announced that they would serve

dinner to all W. people free at another hall. Like Mrs J.
said I have been a good many places where they
served such dinners but I never ate as nice a one.
They had everything one would want and some of the
nicest cakes I ever saw. They seated 103 at the first
table and when we left the hall they had stacks of
eatables yet. In the afternoon the had a very good
program of music, speeches and recitations. I do not
know when I have enjoyed a day more thoroughly
than I did that day. Every one was so friendly and
sociable. It seemed that the folks there could not do
enough for their visitors.

The flowers here are ahead of those there if the
garden is not. The roses have been in bloom over a
week and their very latest ones are blooming now. But
if they are just beginning to bloom there they will be
just right for Childrens Day, June 10, I believe E.
wrote. Hope they will have a good time.
Would like to be there then.

Tell Grandma she must hurry up and get well
for if I do go home soon I do not want to find her sick
yet. Has she tried that Maltine yet or will she take it?

She ought to go to the country and make a visit
when the weather is settled.

I do not know what to say about going home.
Mrs & Mr J. both say I must not think of it, in fact Mr
J. said he would not give 10 cents for my life if I did go
before, I am a good deal better than I am now. The Dr.
said I <u>must</u> not go where it was any <u>lower</u> and it might
be, but he did not think so now; that I would have to
go to a higher climate than this. Sometimes it seems
that I can hardly stand it much longer I want to see
you all so much but perhaps it will be best for me to
stay through this month and may be next. Of course
I'll know more in a few weeks how much good this Dr.

can do me. I have been having a horse back ride every day when it stops raining long enough.

Well I must close and help Mrs J. a little with the dinner. Write as often as you can find time. Love to all

Gertie.

Mrs J. took off 14 little chick this A.M. and has more hatching.

Notes: This was in an envelope addressed to Mrs. B.F. Bice, Elkhart, Illinois. With a postmark from Wellsville, KAS Jun 3 1893. There is a second partial letter in the same envelope which I will include below.

*********************************

Wellsville Kans.

May 4, 1893

Dear Grandma:

Your letter with May's and Gene's, I got when I was in town Tues. and I can tell you I was glad to hear from you all. Sorry that you were not well but hope you are felling much better, now the weather is better.

Mon. it managed to get along without raining and cleared off so that we had some sunshine in the afternoon and Tues. and yesterday were beautiful days, while to-day it is clear most of the time but the wind blows a gale from south. Hope it will not blow up more rain as we had a little shower both yesterday and this noon.

They have not been able to do any farm work yet this week and Mr J. says he is very much afraid the corn will have to be replanted, it was so cold last week. He only has a little in but says he will not plant any more until he know it will grow.

Their garden has not been touched with a hoe
and is at a stand still though this weather would make
it grow fast if it was dry enough so it could be hoed.
Expect Eva and Ma are on

Notes: The rest of the letter is missing but it is in the same
handwriting as the one above from Gertie.
Gertie's mother was Bertha Owen Bice. Gertie was the sister of
Eva Bice Dean. May and Cora were Gertie's sisters. Her Grandma was
Abigail Leach Owen, the mother of Clarence and Mary. Frank and Gene
were Gertie's brothers. Her father, B. F. Bice, had two sisters, Susan and
Sarah. So Aunt S. was probably one of those two. I believe C. is Cora.
Gertie died in 1893.

*******************************

Wellsville Kansas
3 – 4  1903

My dear Sister.
You have my tenderest sympathy
in your great bereavement as I am sure you have, of
every sister in the Circle, I know I cannot say one
word that will comfort you in this sorrow, only that I
think of you, and pray that God will sustain you

Lovingly,

E A Van Meter

*******************************

March 3rd 1903,
Dear Cousin Bertha and family. Today; I
received a card from Cousin May, saying that her
father, Cousin Frank, passed away Sunday morning. I
assure you all that you have our heart-felt sympathys
in your deep sorrow in the loss of a dear father and

husband. While I heard that cousin Frank was sick did not know that he was so seriously ill. Poor May, I feel so sorry for her alone with her babies. Said in her card that they missed cousin "Gene" so much that they "felt that they could not endure it" Arthur has gone out to stay a couple of hours with her tonight I was out about six weeks ago to help her with her sewing. took la grip and could scarcely get home. Sent for the Dr and was in bed very sick for a few days; and have not been able to leave the house since with my lungs like I was in the East. worse than I have ever been since I came West: but I think with care and good weather; will be all right again Just as soon as is safe for me, will go and stay several days with May. Sent for her to come here a few days if Alice was well enough. Suppose Cousin Sue is with you, like an "angel of mercy" that she is, doing quietly more than half dozen other people could do. It was always characteristic of the Bices to to be at home where there was death and sorrow and take hold and do without being told. I often think of cousins "Pick" and Sue and Sallie in every death in our family what a comfort and help they were. And of Cousin Frank, I think the last time I ever saw him, standing by Mothers open grave weeping, and the talk we had before we left the grave concerning the welfare of our Children; and he spoke of Gertie. Now he has joined her; and his <u>dear</u> <u>good</u> mother and a <u>host</u> of others who have <u>not</u> the s---ens that we have. In Gods own good time, <u>we</u> <u>too</u> will lay our burdens down and cross over to be for <u>ever</u> with our loved ones who have left us with aching hearts.

Cousin Bertha; I wish it was in my power to say something that would help you; and each of your Children but <u>words</u> are <u>powerless</u> in such distress. I once thought there was nothing so sad as to give up our friends in death, but there are <u>living</u> troubles far worse than a happy death. A dear friend once said to me just before she died "why its nothing to die" (with a wave of her hand) "just to step over the river and you are at home" How that sweet face and calm manner impressed me, I can never forget it for to her; <u>death had no</u> terrors.

Arthur has just returned from May's. Alice is better, played out doors to day. but Miriam has a cold and was fretful to night Mrs "Stan" and Annie Rand were with May. Must close with love and sympathy for all from myself and Children.

Lovingly Sue & Jeffers

3767 Oseola Street

Notes: These two letters were in the same envelope addressed to Mrs Bertha Bice Wellsville Kansas with a postmark of Denver Highl'ds Mar 6 530PM and a 2 cent stamp.

    May and Gertie were Bertha's daughter and Gene was her son. Arthur Johnson was May's husband and Alice and Miriam (Mim) were their daughters. Bertha's husband was B. F. (Frank) Bice. Bertha also had a son named William Pickrell Bice, who died in 1893. I believe that is who Sue is referring to when she mentions Pick. I have not been able to figure out who Sue and Jeffers are.

********************************

Springfield Ill. March 4, 1903.

Dear Mrs. Bice:

    In yesterday's paper we saw a notice of the death of Mr. Bice. Our thoughts went back to the days in which we were so closely associated with each other – those happy days in Elkhart. Altho' we have been separated from each other the last few years I don't think we have forgotten each other altogether.

Now that another one has been taken from your home we as a family want to send our sympathy. We know how much Mr. Bice will be missed in the home. I wish we could see you and talk it all over but all we can do is to pray for you. You know as well as we do of a comforting heavenly Father. Please send our sympathy to Eva and May as well as the children at home.

I am sorry Eva and I have dropped our correspondence. I think Eva owes me a letter but I suppose she is kept busy with her home duties. I have been home since last Oct. I will return to my work this fall or next spring. You may know I enjoy being home again after several years absence. I feel much better than I did when I just got home. I have enjoyed the winter weather, much to the surprise of all.

I leave tomorrow for a five weeks course of study in the Moody Bible Institute.

I expect to get as far west as Kansas City this summer in visiting churches but don't suppose I can go as far west as your place.

All are well here. Phil was married the last of the year and lives on the farm. We live in town. Papa is talking of making a trip to Idaho this summer.

Laura is still teaching. Frank has three fine boys.

Let us hear from you some time.

Lovingly, Annie E. Sanford

518 S 13th St.

Notes: Annie Sanford was known by Jessie Dean Thackrey's generation and ours as Aunt Annie. She was a close friend of Grandmother Dean – Eva – and became a missionary traveling around the world. She retired as a missionary in India and came to a church sponsored home in Washington, DC. As children we used to visit her.

\*\*\*\*\*\*\*\*\*\*\*\*\*\*\*\*\*\*\*\*\*\*\*\*\*\*\*\*\*\*\*\*\*

Denver, Colo.,
March 5, 1903.

My Dear Mother:

Your note came this morning and the order from Gene. I had not seemed to realize that Father is gone until your note came. Neither can I imagine your loneliness and desolation which will be felt more after Eva and the others are gone. I wish I might come to you then. You will have Gene though, and I know that will be a comfort. Still there is really no help except from One Source and I know you will have that in all its helping and healing power. I wish I might say something to help you but I can not and must be content with telling you I would like to.

I am so sorry Cora is sick but hope a few days rest will do much for her. It seems that I can not express at all what I would like but my heart goes out to you all and I only wish I might be with you for a little while.

Alice is not entirely recovered yet but is better. Since Tuesday I have been going through the same thing with Miriam though she has not been so sick. I used antiflogistine [a topical application used to reduce soreness and swelling] on her throat last night. She seems quite a little better today.

Mrs. Stan has been kindness itself. Alice came up and stayed all night Monday night and Annie Tuesday night. Cousin Sue sent Arthur over as she has been sick with gruppe and we have been having such miserable weather lately that she was afraid to come out.

Tell Gene that Miriam says "Dean" is "done". Mr. Bethel came for his book and wished to be remembered to him. I think I wrote about Smith. Mrs Charles was enquiring about Cora.

139

I was hoping Aunt Sue could remain with you awhile. Do not suppose Maynus could be away from home any great length of time Give my love to both of them I hope some time to see them again

Eva will go home on the train I suppose. I hope she can get settled without the children being sick. I must close as Miriam is becoming restless, with a heart full of love to all.

May.

Notes: This is in an envelope addressed to Mrs. B. F. Bice, Wellsville, Kansas. With a postmark of Denver, Colo. S. Denver Sta. Mar 6 130PM 1903 and a 2 cent stamp.

May is the daughter of B. F. (Frank) Bice and Chloe Bethiah (Bertha) Owen Bice. She is the older sister of Eva Logan Bice. Gene was May's brother and Cora was her sister. Alice and Miriam were her daughters. May married Samuel Arthur Johnson. Miriam was known by many of us as Mim and owned a cabin on the Poudre River with an "infamous" swinging bridge. Aunt Sue was her father's sister.

*********************************

868 Warren Av., Chicago
March 7, 1903

My dear Mrs. Bice and family,

We received a short letter from John last Thursday telling us of your sad loss. We could hardly believe it possible as we did not know of Mr. Bice's sickness.

Our hearts are filled with deepest sympathy for you all in this affliction and with we could have been with you (in) during this time of sorrow.

What a comfort it was to have had Eva at home. Of course it was not possible for May to come home with her little ones recovering from the scarlet fever.

Dear Baby Evelyn will be spared the suffering that you all are undergoing but dear little Bertha will feel it as keenly as a child much older than she for she dearly loved her Grandpapa.

We shall think of you very often and feel most deeply for you and trust that God, the only comforter, will strengthen and support you all under this heavy affliction.

Hoping all are well and with love and deepest sympathy from all, we are,

Most sincerely yours,

Lucia Dean & sisters.

Notes: This was in an envelope addressed to Mrs. Bertha Bice, Wellsville, Kansas and the postmark is from Chicago with a 2 cent stamp.

Eva is Eva Logan Bice Dean and is the daughter of Bertha Owen Bice. "Little" Bertha is Elizabeth Dean and Evelyn is Evelyn Dean Wynne, the two oldest children of Eva and John Dean. Lucia is John G. Dean, Sr's sister. Her sisters were Francis (Frank), Jessie and Emma.

*********************************

[I can't read the location – it is two words and the second looks like either Loma or Iowa]

Aug 11th 1906

Dear Sister Bertha

Your letter recd in due time all were glad to hear from you and that you were all well   I know you are anxious to hear from Sarah so I will see if I cannot get this off on the night mail I think Sarah will write a little if she can lay aside her book long enough   She has been up since eleven and it is now half past five she has been better every other day all the week Monday she did not have any bad spell all

day and was up as much as half the time of course
she was not going to have any more of those spells
was going to get well right away Tuesday she was bad
all day only up a little about five and was up to supper
I think she would have been very comfortable on
Wednesday but she must get up and come out to
breakfast I told her she better keep still 'till she had
her breakfast or she would bring on one of those
spells but no "it will not hurt me one bit I will go slow"
so she came out but could hardly breathe and had no
breath to spare to eat drank some coffee and got back
to the bed I got her shoes off and got her some
whiskey and she had a bad spell and had to stay in
bed 'till noon but she will do the same thing again
when I try to keep her quiet she says "do you think I
can stay in this bed all summer I will never get
strength if I lay here" her mind gits worse I think some
nights she says I have felt so much better today have
not had a bad spell today when she has had two
Thursday night she took such sharp pains through
her heart while at supper just screamed with pain
Hile went for the Dr and stopped for a neighbor on the
way I got hot water as quick as I could and filled the
water bottle was all I could do but guess it was the
right thing she began to get a little easier before the Dr
came it was neuraligia of the heart lasted about an
hour she got easy and rested pretty well all night next
day felt weak and did not get up 'till about three she
certainly grows weaker needs to hold on things when
she walks but those spells are not near as hard and
do not last as long and in the afternoons looks real
bright is very much thinner now when you were here
she is so determined she will get well it may help her
some but I cannot think she will be much better while
she may live a long time perhaps some days she is
sick and is discouraged but not usually   She had a

letter from Eddy last Sat he is in Sanfrancisco at work
for the Santafee it broke her all up cried 'till 1 hr was
so nervous could not keep still I sat on the bed with
her 'till nearly midnight told her she ought to be glad
he had his own way to make and must go where they
send him he said he felt so much better since he was
there "Well I did not want him to go to that God
forsaken place I have lost him" Edd mentioned in his
letter his Father had gone to —ark city and was in the
real estate business and she got it in her head Edd
was going there to  She answered his letter Monday
told him she was going back to Los Angelas this fall
she never could stand the cold winter and she could
get something to do there she thought and if not could
go to the Old Ladies Home  asked if he did not think
that would be the best thing for her to do . Thot
Bertha was going this fall and she could arrange to go
with her  Now Sister you can see how much reason
she has left  We had a earnest talk over her about her
going back and I talked as plain as I could told her
she could never expect to go back she was not able
and had no one to go to and more had not mind
enough to get there if she was able she said Why yes I
can I never thought to stay only 'till fall when I came I
cannot stand the cold would freeze to death I told her
guess she would not freeze by a great fire of course
she is not likely to get able to start if she did you know
how determined she is and if I must say it has not a
grain of sense when she gets her mind made up  I still
keep most [hole in the paper] in hopes I may get the
washing done this week for the first time you asked if I
could not get some one to stay with me I do not know
of any one but if I could I have not the means to pay
for help  I try to save myself all I can lay down and
take a nap every day lay down any way do not always
sleep and I nearly always get my rest at night which

helps me out Hile is pretty well now has Asthma some has gone to the country this afternoon to do a hard job expect he will be back up tonight Bertha the shall come today how nice it is I know you have had a hard time k—thing if Sarah was so pleased and she will tell you for herself I tell her I will not write her part she is now laying down there is a nice breeze today and is very comfortable in the house but the sun is scorching have had healthy warm weather for the last two weeks but the nights have been cool so could get good sleep well I have spread this out quite long enough  close love to all and yourself  the biggest [hole in the paper]

Abby

Notes:  Abby was the wife of Warren Owen, who was the half-brother of Clarence and Mary. Warren apparently died in the late 1860's, though there are records that could indicate he died much later. Not sure if Abby remarried. Sarah could be the Sarah that Mary referred to in her letters back in the early 1870's.

# Chapter 6 — The Poems

Figure 11 — Cover for "Just Before the Battle, Mother"

In addition to the letters that Clarence so faithfully sent to his family, he sent a number of poems as well. Some were in his handwriting, some in an unfamiliar handwriting, and some were typed. Most have been identified. They include:

1. "High Treason Ballad" by Frank Modglin, and sung to the air of "Joe Bowers", and written sometime during the Civil War. Frank was in Capt. James Roper's (successor to Capt. Hall) Company "F", 29th Regiment Illinois Volunteers. (Typed)
2. "Just Before the Battle, Mother", by George F. Root. This was a popular song sung particularly by the Union soldiers during the Civil War. (Handwritten in the same handwriting as a poem attributed to John T. Wright)
3. "Ellsworth's Avengers!", by A.L. Hudson, sung to the tune of "Annie Lisle", and written sometime during the Civil War. (Handwritten in Clarence's handwriting on stationery he usually used)
4. "Faint, Yet Pursuing", from the "Supplemental Tune Book to the Church Sunday School Hymn Book", Judges vitt. 4.

Two poems have not been found in any internet search, and therefore might be original poems. They are included here.

********************************

Graves of the slain composed by John T. Wright on the battle of Murfresboughoro as he was there and help bury the Dead

Blue crimson and white
Were the flowers on that field
Where the brave of our army was lain
They battled to conquer
They never would yield
And we number them now with the slain
2 uncoffined we buried
Them under the sod
Which thier life blood washed to return
Thier patriots spirits commanding to God

Our commander was leader supreme
·3 The few were the tears we shed on thier graves
Yet with grief were our hearts over flowers
As mutely we gazed on the face of the brave
Ere we left them in silence to alone
4 But each bitter tear our eyes did refuse
As we thought of the fate of the morrow
Sank heavy within our sad hearts to in use
With a keener more endureing sorrow
5When slowly we turned from the field of the dead
Thier sad fate many thousand now moan
At homes fare away whence they early had sped
But to which they can never return
6 And now each long night as we stand at our post
There comes to our memory bright
The image of those we've set with the most
In that terreable bloodiest fight
But our cause still in doubt grows dearer to us
Which tis scaled with the blood of the brave
To conquer we come and to conquer we must
Tho we fill a like poviat [?] grave
If we two must feel the keen traitors still
We must follow our flag to the last
For tis better to die for a proud nations weal
Than to live when its glory is past

John T Wright Co F 51st Reg.
Ill Vol Inf Camp Shafer June 23rd 1863

Notes: The spelling throughout the above is the original.

On the same paper and in the same handwriting as "Just Before the Battle, Mother." Neither of these were in the handwriting of Clarence so I am thinking it may have been John Wright's handwriting.

John T. Wright was a Corporal in Company F of the Illinois 51st Infantry Regiment. He was from Mason County, Illinois, which was not far from Williamsville and Elkhart. The 51st was with the 38th a good share of the time from Nashville in Dec. 1862 to Kennesaw Mountain in Jun. 1864, when Corporal Wright was killed Jun. 27, 1864. It is nowhere explained why the poem was in Clarence's possession.

*********************************

## THE SOLDIER'S RETURN,
IN DISGUISE.

By D. D. Fisher, 1st Batt., Pioneer Brigade, Army of the Cumberland.

Air, "Mollie Bond"

Lady, should I meet thee ever,
At some social circle, where
I could have an introduction
To a damsel neat and fair.

Chorus.

Soldier, welcome, welcome home.
(Repeat.)

Notwithstanding we are strangers,
There's one boon I ask of thee,
That my pleasures may be doubled,
And my heart would then be free.

Stranger in the garden walking
Singing songs of melody,
Naught on earth could give me pleasure,
But to come and walk with thee.

Lady, do not deem me foolish,
I have naught to ask beside,
But that thou would ever love me

And consent to be my bride.

Sir, I could not love another
Other than a soldier true,
Fighting for our country's freedom,
For the Red, the White, the Blue.

Leave me, stranger, no more questions
Will I answer unto thee.
Go and fight like other patriots,
For thy Country's liberty.

Lady, since thou cannot love me,
All my hopes and joys are fled,
On the battle-field there's honor, --
Would I were among the dead.

Stay one moment, be contented,
Lady, stay, oh! Do not fear;
Hear my story all unravelled,
It will cost thee but a tear.

Lady, I have been a soldier,
Fighting for our liberty;
Fought in battles on Stone River,
In the State of Tennessee.

There it was I saw your lover,
Sword in hand, our flag his shield,
And his thoughts on thee, fair lady,
Gave him courage on the field.

We were out on New Year's morning,
Ordered out to take the field,
By our bold and brave commander,
Who had sworn to never yield.

Soon the balls flew thick around us,
And the cannons loud did roar;
But we drove the foe before us
And they could not rally more.

But, alas! Why art thou weeping?
Is it for that absent one?
Never more can'st thou behold him,
For his mortal race is run.

He was brave, yes, bold and fearless,
Never thinking for to yield;
But the murderous gun hath slain him,
He was buried on the field.

He is gone where sin and sorrow
Is not felt nor feared no more,
Far beyond war's desolation
And the cannon's solemn roar.

Lady, dry those tears of sorrow,
Listen to the song I'll sing;
It will give thee joy and comfort,
And perhaps glad tidings bring.

Leave me, stranger, ever leave me;
I no more can pleasure know;
All my joys are turned to sorrow,
To the battle-field I'll go.

There erect my lover's tombstone,
Lay me down and die in peace;
Bid farewell to worldly pleasure,
Sing the songs that never cease.

Lady, true; no angel truer,
Oh, forgive me of the wrong;
See the sorrow I have caused thee,
Now I'll sing another song.

Dear one, I had thought to test thee,
Now I find there's none so true,
In disguise I have deceived thee,
But my love's the same to you.

Fair one, thou doth seem to doubt me,
Could I not be recognized
By a friend, yea, more, a lover?
Read my meaning in mine eyes.

See, oh, see, this ring you gave me;
A token of the love you bore,
Showing that you would remember
Me when I returned from war.

Now the time has come to leave thee,
But I soon will call again,
And I never more will grieve thee,
Blessings rest upon thy name.

Fortune smiles when sorrow nears us,
Nature has ordained it so,
God has spared our nation's honor,
Never more to war we'll go.

Notes: This one was typed, rather than in handwriting.

David D. Fisher was a Sergeant in the 1st Battalion of The Pioneer Brigade of the Army of the Cumberland. The Pioneer Brigade was in Nashville, Murfreesboro, Chattanooga, Kennesaw Mountain, and Atlanta at the same time as the 38th. It is nowhere explained why the poem was in Clarence's possession.

# Appendix — Genealogy

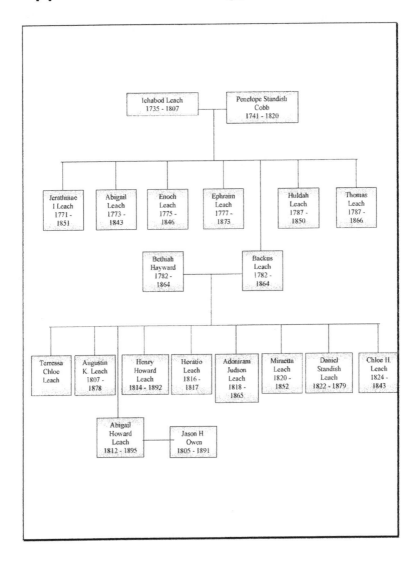

Figure 12 — Family of Ichabod Leach and Penelope Standish

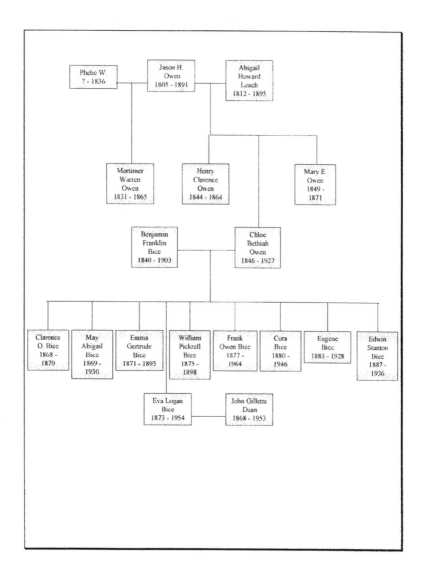

**Figure 13 — Family of Jason Owen and Abigail Leach**

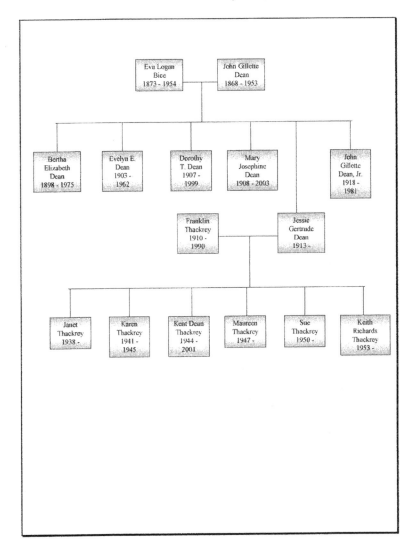

**Figure 14 — Family of Eva Bice and John Dean**

# Bibliography

Alden Kindred of America, Inc. *Descendants of John Alden*
  http://www.alden.org/aldgen
Historical Data Systems, comp. *American Civil War Soldiers* [database
  on-line]. Provo, UT, USA: The Generations Network, Inc.,
  1999. Copyright 1997-2000. Historical Data Systems, Inc.
Historical Data Systems, comp.. *U.S. Civil War Soldier Records and
  Profiles* [database on-line]. Provo: The Generations Network,
  Inc., 2009. Copyright 1997-2009. Historical Data Systems, Inc.
National Park Service. *Civil War Soldiers and Sailor System*
  http://www.itd.nps.gov/cwss/regiments.cfm
Robert I. Girardi and Nathaniel Cheairs Hughes, Jr., editors. *The
  Memoirs of Brigadier General William Passmore Carlin,
  U.S.A.*, Lincoln: University of Nebraska Press, 1999.

**Photo Credits:**

Cover: Collection of Owen Family letters and envelopes, by Maureen
Thackrey Lischke.
Title Page: Bertha Owen Bice and her family, taken from publicly
available photo on www.ancestry.com, originally submitted by
Michael Colgate. Pictured in photo, from left to right, are Edwin Bice,
Jesse Collins, Helen Bice (seated in lap), Gene Bice, Elizabeth Dean,
Evelyn Dean, Lillian Tombs Bice (in back), Owen Bice, Chloe "Bertha"
Owen Bice, Bice Johnson, Miriam Johnson, Cora Bice Collins, Frank
Bice, and Hazel Bice (seated in lap).
Introduction: Elkhart Cemetery, by Sue Thackrey and Keith Richards
Thackrey

# Index

*From left to right: Keith Thackrey, Sue Thackrey (sister) and Maureen Thackrey Lischke*

## ABOUT THE AUTHORS

The actual Owen family letters came into the possession of Maureen Thackrey Lischke through the death of her aunt. She transcribed the letters and annotated them with notes explaining events and relationships. Her brother Keith Thackrey compiled the letters into their present form, adding genealogical research, as well as the introduction and preface. Keith has performed considerable genealogical research through ancestry.com and through a variety of personal and public sources. They have both conducted field research at, among other places, Elkhart, Illinois; Lebanon and Eaton, New York; and Wellsville, Kansas. Maureen and Keith are the great grandchildren of Bertha Owen, and the great-great grandchildren of Jason and Abigail Owen, the recipients of the Owen family letters.

Maureen and her husband Erv live on an alpaca ranch in Victor, Montana. Keith lives with his wife Jeanie and their two daughters, Kit and Rebecca, in Falls Church, Virginia. They are both retired civil servants.

Made in the USA
Charleston, SC
21 September 2012